DISARMED

WHAT THE UKRAINE WAR TEACHES AMERICANS ABOUT THE RIGHT TO BEAR ARMS

MARK W. SMITH

BOMBARDIER

Published by Bombardier Books
An Imprint of Post Hill Press
ISBN: 978-1-63758-923-6
ISBN (eBook): 978-1-63758-924-3

Disarmed:
What the Ukraine War Teaches Americans About the Right to Bear Arms
© 2023 by JBHB 1985 LLC
All Rights Reserved

No part of this book may be reproduced, stored in a retrieval system, or transmitted by any means without the written permission of the author and publisher.

Post Hill Press
New York • Nashville
posthillpress.com

Published in the United States of America
1 2 3 4 5 6 7 8 9 10

Also by Mark W. Smith

#Duped: How the Anti-gun Lobby Exploits the Parkland School Shooting—and How Gun Owners Can Fight Back

First They Came for the Gun Owners: The Campaign to Disarm You and Take Your Freedoms

CONTENTS

1: Ukraine: The Ultimate Real-Life
   Lesson in the Dangers of Disarming Citizens   1

2: The U.S. Can't Repeat Ukraine's Mistakes   19

3: Too Little, and Nearly Too Late: Paying the Price for
   Failing to Protect the Individual Right to Bear Arms   33

4: Yes, Small Arms Matter—a Lot   55

5: The Deterrence Factor (or: Why Tyrants Disarm the People)   93

6: The Doomsday Provision   123

Endnotes   141

About the Author   213

1

UKRAINE: THE ULTIMATE REAL-LIFE LESSON IN THE DANGERS OF DISARMING CITIZENS

Anti-gun crusaders in the United States often insist that the Second Amendment's individual right to keep and bear arms is a "relic."[1]

They should try telling that to the people of Ukraine.

You see, Ukraine doesn't have an equivalent to the Second Amendment. Nothing in its constitution protects the right to keep and bear arms. And the country had restrictive gun laws for decades. It loosened them (somewhat) only hours before Russia invaded in February 2022.

Do you think Ukrainians regret those previous decisions now?

Ask the tens of thousands of Ukrainians who rushed out to buy guns before the invasion, stocking up on AR-15 rifles and other firearms that American gun-control activists insist "no one needs."[2]

Aptly known as "America's Rifle," the AR-15 and like rifles are the ultimate defensive arms for civilians.³

Or ask the Ukrainian parliament, which at the last minute passed the law allowing civilians—finally—to carry guns and act in self-defense.⁴

Or ask Ukraine's president, who told the people: "We will give weapons to anyone who wants to defend the country. Be ready to support Ukraine in the squares of our cities."⁵

Or ask the millions of Ukrainians (including great-grandmothers)⁶ who answered the call—whether by lining up to receive automatic weapons the government handed out, joining armed militias, firing rifles at Russian armored vehicles, making Molotov cocktails and hurling them at invading forces, patrolling their cities with no body armor and with whatever weapons they could get their hands on, shooting at enemy drones, or setting up armed checkpoints.⁷

Many experts would have told you before the invasion that all this effort was a waste of time and lives. How could civilians with small arms expect to stop one of the world's most powerful militaries, a military with nuclear weapons? The chairman of the U.S. Joint Chiefs of Staff said he expected the Russians to take Kyiv, Ukraine's capital, within seventy-two hours.⁸

That kind of thinking shouldn't surprise Americans. Americans hear it regularly from anti-gun politicians in the United States, who scoff at the idea that armed citizens can do anything useful against today's heavily armed, sophisticated militaries.

Take Joe Biden. The president has said, dismissively: "For those brave right-wing Americans who say [the Second Amendment is] all about keeping America independent and safe, if you want to fight against the country, you need an F-15 [fighter jet]. You need something more than a gun."[9] (As shown in Chapter 4, President Biden trots out this talking point a lot.)

Or take Eric Swalwell, a California congressman who was (for about five minutes) a candidate for the Democrats' 2020 presidential nomination.[10] In 2018, Representative Swalwell wrote an op-ed in *USA Today* calling for a ban on the sale *and* possession of "assault weapons" (which is a scary propaganda term for ordinary civilian semiautomatic rifles). The headline even said that the United States should "go after resisters."[11] Someone on Twitter wrote: "So basically [Swalwell] wants a war. Because that's what you would get." The Twitter user said anyone is crazy "if you think I'll give up my rights and give the gov[ernment] all the power." Representative Swalwell's response: "And it would be a short war my friend. The government has nukes."[12]

The Founders, of course, were advocates of armed citizen-soldiers, believing that standing armies in times of peace are dangerous. And now we have a president of the United States and a member of the House of Representatives threatening American citizens with the powerful weapons of a huge standing army.

I hope that President Biden, Representative Swalwell, and other gun prohibitionists paid attention to what Ukrainian civilians have done with small arms to resist the Russians. But I doubt it: Biden made his comment about needing F-15s six months into the war in Ukraine. That was long after Ukrainians with little or no military training helped to drive Russian forces out of the approaches to Kyiv, the city that Vladimir Putin was supposed to take in seventy-two hours.[13]

The most zealous anti-gun activists may be immune to facts, logic, and evidence. But many other people aren't.

That's why I have written this book: to call attention to the vital lessons that Ukraine's story teaches—*if we bother to notice them.*

After Ukraine passed the law protecting the people's right to carry firearms, the chairman of the nation's parliament declared that the act's purpose was "to ensure that every citizen receives the sacred right to self-defense."[14] But why did Ukraine wait so long to protect this "sacred right"? Only an imminent invasion by a mighty military force woke up the country's leaders.

Will the United States learn from Ukraine's mistakes? Our country is blessed to have a Constitution that protects the fundamental right to keep and bear arms. And yet prominent American leaders now crusade to subvert the "sacred right to self-defense." Many of the same politicians who have rushed to arm Ukrainians want to disarm Americans. We'll discuss some probable reasons for that later in this book.

As a result, some Americans are poised to give away *our* gun rights, while Ukrainians suffer the consequences of not having protected *their* rights. Unless America wakes up to the dangers of this approach, we may find ourselves in a situation like that of the Ukrainians—paying a steep price for failing to protect the right to armed self-defense.

Ukraine's experience offers the ultimate real-life lesson in why a free people must preserve the right to keep and bear arms, even in the 21st century.

Ordinary Citizens Protect Their Communities and Their Country

In March 2022, early in the invasion, Russian troops bombarded the Ukrainian city of Chernihiv. According to the State Border Service of Ukraine, a seventy-two-year-old man living in the city grabbed his rifle and fired at a Russian Su-34 jet flying low overhead. The retiree's shots "targeted and destroyed" the $50 million supersonic fighter-bomber, Ukrainian officials said. Ukraine awarded this gentleman a medal and hailed him as a hero.[15]

This would be a remarkable story directly refuting Joe Biden's claims—if it were true. Alas, it seems exceedingly unlikely that a rifle shot could take down a supersonic aircraft. The story is probably a propaganda piece.

But here's the thing: Such propaganda (if it is indeed that) is unnecessary. Civilians made remarkable contributions to the Ukrainian cause from the beginning, as this book demonstrates.

There were plenty of heroes—bank employees, taxi drivers, teachers, IT professionals, mayors, and many others. That's the power of an armed citizenry.

One Ukrainian buying a pump-action shotgun before the invasion said that he knew he couldn't "stop the Russians" with his weapon. So why arm himself? He said, "I want to protect my house from looters."[16] It turned out to be a valid concern: Putin's forces have looted homes and businesses across Ukraine.[17]

This Ukrainian citizen was right: one person with a gun won't take down a whole army, but he *can* protect his home and his family.

Meanwhile, a bunch of people with guns can protect their community.

And if enough citizens across the nation are armed and have decent training? At the very least, they can slow down an invading army. They can even help to defeat it.

Many books about the Second Amendment and armed citizens tend to focus on the use of firearms for defense of self, family, and home from criminal violence, or on the use of firearms for lawful purposes such as hunting, competitive shooting, and recreational shooting. Some may touch on the need for armed citizens to be able to resist mob violence, riots, and looting. While recognizing the legitimacy of such uses, this book focuses on the need for an armed, trained citizenry in the event of larger scale disasters, such as a foreign invasion or other actions by a foreign power, like China, or to prevent domestic oppression, or possible civil unrest. All of these would be disasters of the first magnitude, and no sane person wants them to happen. But these kinds of events sometimes do happen.

As you'll see in this book, Ukraine's experience provides ample evidence that armed citizens can and do figure prominently in a nation's defense. That's the good news. The bad news is that Ukraine made many mistakes that put the country in a dangerous position in which it never needed to be. Whatever successes Ukrainians achieved occurred despite their leaders' previous errors.

The emergency decision to arm citizens clearly helped Ukraine's cause, but that decision came way too late. By waiting until the eleventh hour to prepare, Ukraine's leaders left their soldiers and civilians scrambling to mount a defense. Volunteer units had begun training on their own years earlier, but Ukraine didn't incorporate them into the country's defenses until weeks before the invasion.[18] Gun stores sold out quickly because so many Ukrainians rushed to buy firearms, all at the last moment.[19] Arms supplies proved so insufficient that volunteers needed to donate their guns to professional soldiers.[20] Ukrainian forces, both volunteers and those in the regular army, ran low on ammunition.[21] Ukraine might have avoided some of these shortfalls if it hadn't destroyed a huge stockpile of weapons and ammunition it already possessed—a story explored in Chapter 2. Some Ukrainian civilians, desperate to learn how to handle firearms, trained using cardboard, plastic, or wooden replicas of guns.[22] The photos of this training could have been a parody by *The Babylon Bee*. Unfortunately, these photos reflected the dangerous and depressing reality that years of unpreparedness by the Ukrainian government had brought upon its citizens.

The Ukrainians learned a lesson that people around the world need to understand: contrary to what gun-control crusaders claim, you can never have "too many" guns or "too much" ammunition.

Shortly after the invasion, a writer for *The Atlantic* claimed that the Ukrainians had "failed badly" by "waiting too long to arm and train their citizens." He added, "If you want ordinary people to make your society occupation-proof, you have to teach them to kill well before they need to do so."[23] Bingo!

The Atlantic is not exactly a mouthpiece for the gun-rights movement. Now owned by Steve Jobs's widow, *The Atlantic* mostly serves as a bull horn for the typical left-leaning political, social, and cultural views of America's urban elites.

A military analyst and historian of guerrilla warfare didn't wait until after the fact to point out Ukraine's mistakes. He sounded the alarm more than two months before Russia invaded. Referring to the possibilities of "arming the Ukrainian people" and "waging guerrilla warfare," he asked, "Why wait for a Russian invasion to make these preparations?" Then he said, "The Ukrainian government needs to start distributing weapons now."[24]

But Ukraine didn't do it.

The failure to arm civilians or organize volunteer forces sooner proved costly on two levels. Most obviously, it left Ukrainians in a mad rush to figure out how to stop the Russians. They could have started preparing much earlier had their leaders not clung to the gun-control mindset. But just as important, Ukraine robbed itself of the *deterrence factor*. As this book will show, a well-armed populace can make would-be invaders or tyrants (or terrorists or criminals) think twice about trying to take control.

So, what should Americans take away from seeing Ukrainians rush to arm themselves at the last minute? *Never, ever allow this country to be disarmed.* Then we won't need to worry about how quickly and how much the people can be armed when danger is imminent.

Civilians with Small Arms Make a Big Impact

Now, you might look at Ukraine's defense against Russia and think, *Who cares what some civilians did? What matters is that the United States and other countries sent them billions of dollars' worth of heavy weapons and other military aid.*

But that perspective misses the mark for several reasons.

First, civilians with small arms played a crucial role in standing up to Russian forces, especially during the critical early periods of the war (as Chapter 4 will show).

Second, much of that foreign aid came in the form of small arms and ammunition—thousands of guns and many millions of rounds of ammo.[25]

Third, while foreign military aid is critically important, it doesn't ensure success. Look at all the money the United States poured into arming and training Afghans. Only six weeks before U.S. troops withdrew from Afghanistan, President Joe Biden assured Americans that the U.S. had given the Afghans "all the tools, training, and equipment of any modern military."[26] So what happened as soon as the United States pulled out? The Taliban rolled over the Afghan government forces and took control of the country within days. Similarly, Muslim guerrillas in Afghanistan defeated the mighty Soviet army in the 1980s.

And that leads to the fourth point: Why do you think the United States and other countries keep sending military aid to Ukraine? Because Ukrainians—both military and civilians—are putting up a fierce resistance. They are willing to fight and had success doing so. By contrast, Biden acknowledged that Afghans "collapsed, sometimes without trying to fight."[27] (Just weeks earlier, Biden had insisted it was "highly unlikely" you'd see the Taliban "overrunning everything and owning the whole country."[28] Whoops!)

One can't overstate the importance of how armed civilians, determined to protect their homes, contributed to Ukraine's defense. There are many historical precedents where overmatched forces have repeatedly held strong against—and have even defeated—powerful militaries. How? The underdogs are highly motivated and use the techniques of irregular warfare.

John Stark, who led American revolutionary forces in the Battles of Bennington and Bunker Hill, once explained the success of his troops this way: "our 'astonishing success' taught the enemies of liberty that undisciplined freemen are superior to veteran slaves."[29]

Why an armed people fight can be more important than *what weaponry* they fight with.

The eminent French author, journalist, and philosopher Bernard-Henri Lévy has made this point. Lévy traveled to Ukrainian war zones five times in the first eight months after the Russian invasion. In October 2022 he told *The Wall Street Journal* that "the real reason Putin has not succeeded"—and the reason why Ukrainians maintained high morale even though Russians had committed "stomach-churning" atrocities against civilians—is that Ukrainians "know why they fight." Specifically, they fight not merely for "their existence, their survival," but also for "values which they believe are worth risking their lives for."[30]

Preparedness

The situation in Ukraine is a reminder that ordinary civilians may be called to defend their homes, communities, or nation at a moment's notice. So, it's essential to prepare.

Of course, you might dismiss the idea that the United States could be invaded. A despot like Putin doesn't live across the border and harbor aggressive designs on our country. And many factors would make an invasion of America extraordinarily difficult to pull off—the geography (protected by two oceans), the sheer size of the country, the strength of the U.S. military, and, yes, a well-armed population of more than 330 million.[31]

But consider a few other points.

First, even if you doubt that an invasion is possible, many other Americans disagree. A September 2022 YouGov poll revealed that nearly a third of Americans believe that the United States could be invaded within the next decade.[32]

Second, history is full of events that, before they happened, seemed unlikely or even impossible. Before 1914, who would have thought the assassination of the heir to the Austro-Hungarian throne could have plunged the world into war? Four mighty empires that existed when World War I began—Austro-Hungarian, Ottoman, German, and Russian—were gone by the war's end.[33] No one foresaw such a widespread collapse. Nassim Nicholas Taleb chronicled the outsized impact of highly improbable events in his bestselling book *The Black Swan*. Taleb characterized Black Swan occurrences as rare, unpredictable events for which, after the fact, we concoct explanations to make them seem explainable and predictable.[34] Black Swans have had a huge influence on the course of history, and many of these events are negative (think 9/11 or World War I).

Third, the U.S. faces many potential threats beyond a traditional land invasion. On the international level, China wouldn't need to mount a D-Day-style invasion of North America. In 2021, China tested a hypersonic missile that circled the globe.[35] Senior U.S. officials have admitted that the United States "failed miserably" in war-gaming exercises involving China.[36] And the director of the U.S. Strategic Command, Admiral Charles Richard, has warned: "As I assess our level of deterrence against China, the ship is slowly sinking. It is sinking slowly, but it is sinking, as fundamentally they [the Chinese] are putting capability in the field faster than we are." The admiral said that China's new advantages amount to "a very near-term problem." He concluded: "The big one is coming. And it isn't going to be very long before we're going to get tested in ways that we haven't been tested [for] a long time."[37]

If the Chinese wanted to disrupt the American homeland, they could take down the whole electrical grid with electromagnetic pulses (EMPs). Or they could use cyberattacks and localized sabotage to cripple water supplies, electricity, and fuel distribution. Any of these scenarios could lead to chaos and lawlessness. And let's not forget how China flew a surveillance balloon across the entire continental United States in February 2023.[38]

But we don't need a foreign enemy to create chaos in the United States.

A *Washington Post*/ABC News poll from late 2022 showed that nearly 90 percent of Americans are concerned about the growing risk of political violence.[39] The problem has become so bad that 37 percent of Americans feel that a civil war is at least somewhat likely within the next decade, according to the September 2022 YouGov poll that showed a fear of invasion. And 47 percent believe the same about a "total economic collapse."⁴⁰ Such a collapse would dramatically increase the chances of looting, violence, and social chaos.

In other words, make sure you have plenty of guns and ammo handy.

That preparedness is the best way I know to ensure the kind of "robustness" or resilience that Taleb calls for when Black Swan events arise. Having arms and ammunition, the training to use them, and the legal right to use them—that's the most effective defense against tyranny and terror no matter what form they take.

Yet influential figures in the United States want to bar civilians from having access to entire classes of guns. They want to make it as difficult as possible for average citizens to buy firearms. And even if a civilian can purchase a weapon, gun-control crusaders want to keep that person from carrying the firearm outside his home. Their ultimate dream is to confiscate guns altogether.

This is the opposite of preparedness. Implementing these steps would leave you unready to defend yourself, your family, and your community.

Another key element of preparedness is the willingness to fight, something that Ukrainians have put on full display. Are Americans similarly motivated to defend their country? A poll conducted shortly after Russia's February 2022 invasion of Ukraine should concern you. The survey asked Americans, "If you were in the same position as Ukrainians are now, do you think that you would stay and fight or leave the country?" More eighteen- to thirty-four-year-olds said they'd leave the country (48 percent) than said they'd stay and fight (45 percent). That's a scary statement from the population you'd expect to serve as the heart of America's defenses.⁴¹

Threats and Deterrence

In the nineteenth century, the great Supreme Court justice and constitutional scholar Joseph Story captured the importance of an armed citizenry when he said it stands as "the natural defence of a free country against sudden foreign invasions, domestic insurrections, and domestic usurpations of power by rulers."⁴²

Ukraine demonstrates the dangers of both foreign invasion and domestic insurrection. Years before Putin's tanks rolled into Ukraine, Russia backed a separatist movement that arose in the Donbas region of eastern Ukraine. The insurrectionists attracted enough Russian sympathizers, and enough Russian support, to set up puppet governments in two provinces there, Donetsk and Luhansk.⁴³

Now think about the United States. Remember the 2020 riots that the media described as "mostly peaceful protests"?⁴⁴ The riots claimed at least nineteen lives in just a two-week stretch in late May and early June 2020.⁴⁵ More than seven hundred law enforcement officers were injured.⁴⁶ In the same period, all the riots, arson, and looting caused between $1 billion and $2 billion in property damage.⁴⁷

But, do you know what was really striking about these events? In cities such as Chicago, Portland, and Minneapolis, local leaders refused to cooperate with federal law enforcement to quell the riots.[48] In effect, they encouraged lawlessness. The lack of response revealed an important lesson: the government and law enforcement will not always be there to protect you. The founder of the National African American Gun Association, Philip Smith, told CNN that the group's membership soared in 2020. "To me," Smith said, "the pandemic was the line in the sand for a lot of folks that were even anti-gun, because the pandemic made you realize that you may not have food in your cabinet, there might be social unrest, there might be mob violence."[49]

He's right. Giving up your right to self-defense is a terrible idea.

You don't need to envision hypothetical scenarios to see why. As discussed in Chapter 5, every day we face real dangers—gangs, illegal aliens, high-crime areas, mob violence, states where laws restrict your right to keep and bear arms, and more.

Don't kid yourself: The world is a dangerous place. Saying "it won't happen to me" is naive and reckless.

So is saying "it can't happen here." Many Ukrainians never expected to be fighting for their lives and their country. Even with Putin mounting troops on the border, Ukraine's president expressed doubts that Russia would invade.[50]

Putting their heads in the sand didn't do anything to deter the threat or fight it once the invasion began.

And how about "domestic usurpations of power"? Those can certainly happen in the United States. They already have, in fact.

Think about all state and local leaders who invoked "emergency powers" to shut down schools and businesses starting in 2020. They typically did it by executive order, sometimes defying legislators. And many leaders extended their "emergency powers" indefinitely. It's no accident that in 2021, at least forty-seven states introduced measures to give legislatures more oversight of executive actions.[51]

Such power grabs trample the freedoms of citizens like you and me. And we're seeing them occur more and more.

Heed Ukraine's Warnings

George Packer is an award-winning reporter for *The Atlantic* and, previously, for *The New Yorker*. He wrote a bestselling book about the Iraq War.[52] When Russia invaded Ukraine in 2022, Packer went to Ukraine to see what was happening.

Packer is no conservative or gun-rights activist. In fact, the ultra-liberal magazine *The Nation* says, "For more than two decades, he has been among this country's leading liberal commentators."[53] But what he saw in Ukraine had him uttering thoughts you don't typically hear from pro-gun-control liberals in the United States.

In September 2022, Packer wrote a long essay for *The Atlantic* based on his on-the-ground reporting. The piece carried the headline "Ukrainians Are Defending the Values Americans Claim to Hold."[54]

Packer wrote: "A tyrannical Goliath was trying to kill a democratic David. That's why Ukraine was worth the risk. Anyone with a human heartbeat who came and saw knew it." Packer met a Navy veteran from Chicago named Rom Stevens, who had traveled to Ukraine to volunteer. Stevens told him the Ukrainians were "fighting for an ideal"—to "determine their own government, their religion, their culture." Another veteran who went to Ukraine, a Green Beret from Texas named Ramiro Carrasco Jr., told Packer: "Slaves can never defeat free people—it can never happen. Putin made a big mistake. He didn't know these people. Once a man tastes the taste of freedom, he won't let anyone take it from him."[55] Here's how Packer responded to these comments:

> *I didn't know what these men thought of American politics, and I didn't want to know. Back home we might have argued; we might have detested each other. Here, we were joined by a common belief in what the Ukrainians were trying to do and admiration for how they were doing it. Here, all the complex infighting and chronic disappointments and sheer lethargy of any democratic society, but especially ours, dissolved, and the essential things—to be free and live with dignity—became clear.*[56]

Then Packer offered this kicker: "It almost seemed as if the U.S. would have to be attacked or undergo some other catastrophe for Americans to remember what Ukrainians have known from the start."[57]

That's the scenario this book is designed to help us avoid.

2

THE U.S. CAN'T REPEAT UKRAINE'S MISTAKES

Learn from other people's mistakes as much as possible.
—Warren Buffett

If you're wondering what to learn from Ukraine's experience, remember this old saying: it's good to learn from your own mistakes, but it's much better to learn from *other people's* mistakes.

You can bet that many Ukrainians regret their country's long-standing negative approach to firearms and the right to bear arms. The country made mistake after mistake over the course of decades and resisted opportunities to correct those errors.

Ukrainians have learned their lesson about private gun rights the hard way. Americans can't let the same thing happen. Otherwise, we risk losing our freedom.

So, let's learn from Ukraine's biggest mistakes.

Mistake #1: No Equivalent to the Second Amendment's Right to Bear Arms

Ukraine's failure to protect the people's right to keep and bear arms left the country vulnerable. At a minimum, it prevented the Ukrainians—military and civilians—from putting up the strongest defense possible when the Russians invaded on February 24, 2022. And as we'll see in Chapter 5, had Ukraine installed robust protections for the right to keep and bear arms, that move might have deterred a Russian invasion.

Ukraine scrambled at the last minute to try to undo its mistakes, but the changes came too late.

Although Ukraine broke away from the Soviet Union in 1991, the Soviet tradition of severe regulation of private firearms endured in the newly independent nation.[58] Ukrainians had more than thirty years to correct this problem before the Russian invasion. Alas, they didn't do it.

Ten years ago, they had a perfect chance to fix the problem, too.

Ukraine adopted its constitution in 1996. That constitution allows the Ukrainian parliament to pass amendments by a two-thirds vote. The parliament has done just that on many occasions—in 2004, 2011, 2013, 2014, 2016, and 2019.[59]

About a decade before Russia invaded, a movement developed in Ukraine calling for Second Amendment–type protections. How do we know that Ukraine became interested in securing gun rights? Because the country's leading constitutional law journal reached out to two of the most prominent Second Amendment scholars in the United States: Stephen P. Halbrook and Joyce Lee Malcolm.

If you're looking for top Second Amendment scholars, you can't do much better than Halbrook and Malcolm. Halbrook, who holds both a PhD and a law degree, is an attorney who has argued and won three firearm-related cases before the U.S. Supreme Court. He has written several important books on the Second Amendment and gun restrictions, including *The Right to Bear Arms*, *The Founders' Second Amendment*, *America's Rifle: The Case for the AR-15*, and *Gun Control in the Third Reich*. Halbrook's scholarly work has appeared in such publications as the *Harvard Journal of Law and Public Policy* and the *Georgetown Journal of Law and Public Policy*.[60]

Malcolm, meanwhile, is a historian and constitutional scholar who is professor emerita at George Mason University's Antonin Scalia Law School. Malcolm has written two groundbreaking books (both published by Harvard University Press) on Anglo-American gun rights, gun control, and violence.[61] Her most important work is likely her book entitled *To Keep and Bear Arms: The Origins of an Anglo-American Right*.

But probably the greatest testament to Halbrook and Malcolm's influence is that the Supreme Court has relied on their scholarship when ruling on the Second Amendment. Most notably, the Court cited Halbrook and Malcolm in the landmark 2008 decision *District of Columbia v. Heller*. This ruling affirmed that the Second Amendment protects an individual right to keep and bear arms.[62]

So, you can see why Ukraine's leading law journal turned to these American scholars and asked them to submit papers. The journal published Second Amendment articles by Halbrook and Malcolm in 2013.[63]

Now, you might be thinking, *What's the big deal about a couple of articles in a law journal?* But it is a big deal. This is the leading legal journal in Ukraine, read by the country's legal elites. It's been around for a century.[64] And these Second Amendment articles appeared during a time of upheaval. Only a year later, the Ukrainian parliament voted to oust the pro-Russian president, Viktor Yanukovych.[65] Ukraine also passed constitutional amendments in 2011, 2013, and 2014. The point is, from a constitutional perspective, many options were on the table.

And more and more Ukrainians wanted their country to follow America's example with the Second Amendment. Halbrook recalls: "Support was growing for liberalized gun laws at that time. The Ukrainian Gun Owners Association and some political parties were demanding action."[66]

In fact, Ukrainians proposed such a constitutional amendment in 2014. The leader of parliament, Oleksandr Turchynov, introduced an amendment that included three clauses:

1. All able-bodied citizens are required to receive military training.

2. Every citizen has the right to defend his constitutional rights against usurpations of power or encroachments on Ukraine's sovereignty.

3. "Every citizen of Ukraine has the right to possess firearms to protect his life and health, house and property, the life and health of others, constitutional rights and freedoms in case of usurpation of power, and encroachments on the constitutional order, sovereignty and territorial integrity of Ukraine."[67] The exercise of the right to own a firearm is governed by applicable law and may be limited only by a court order concerning an individual.[68]

Turchynov proposed this amendment almost immediately after the parliament ousted Ukraine's pro-Russia president. The petition for the gun-rights amendment reached "the required number of signatures in record time," according to the Ukrainian Gun Owners Association.[69]

Only days later, Russia invaded Crimea. Soon Putin annexed that Ukrainian peninsula.[70] In Halbrook's words, "Russia's military annexation of Crimea brought the reform efforts to a halt, and the proposed constitutional amendment was not acted on."[71]

Of course, Russia's actions clearly signaled its aggressive intentions. Another indication came soon thereafter, in July 2014, when pro-Russian forces used Russian weapons to shoot down Malaysia Airlines Flight 17 over Ukraine.[72]

But Ukraine still didn't provide constitutional protection for the right to keep and bear arms. The consequences of that failure become painfully clear later.

It shouldn't have taken Russia's invasion to reveal the importance of an armed citizenry. If Ukrainians wanted to follow the U.S. example, they should have looked to the wisdom of America's Founders.

None other than the Father of the Constitution explained the essential nature of the right to keep and bear arms. In *Federalist* No. 46, James Madison pointed out an "advantage" Americans held "over the people of almost every other nation." What was it? "The advantage of being armed," he wrote. Madison drew a contrast with governments in Europe, which were "afraid to trust the people with arms."[73]

Most European governments still are afraid. Or in the case of Ukraine, they *were* until it was almost too late.

Another important figure from the early American republic explained why an armed citizenry acts as a vital protection against foreign invasion—like the one Russia launched on Ukraine.

The man I'm talking about is Joseph Story. He may not be as well-known as James Madison, but he has had a huge influence on American constitutional thought.

Who was Joseph Story? Among other things, he was the youngest justice ever appointed to the Supreme Court. He was only thirty-two when, in 1811, President Madison nominated him. Story was also one of the longest-tenured justices in U.S. history. He served on the Court for thirty-three years during a vital period in the American republic's formation. During that time, he wrote many significant opinions.[74] One of his best-known opinions came in the case *United States v. The Amistad*. Writing for the Court, Justice Story granted freedom to the enslaved Africans who had carried out a mutiny aboard the slave ship *Amistad*.[75] Steven Spielberg made a movie about the case.

Amazingly, though, Joseph Story's tenure on the Supreme Court may not be the most important part of his legacy. What matters more? His work as a constitutional scholar. Even while serving on the Supreme Court, Story spent many years as a law professor at Harvard. He also wrote authoritative treatises on the law. The most influential is his *Commentaries on the Constitution of the United States*.[76] To this day, Story's *Commentaries* stands as a definitive source for understanding the Constitution from an originalist perspective. The book is right up there with the essays by James Madison, Alexander Hamilton, and John Jay in *The Federalist*. That's how important Story's writings are.

In Chapter 1, you saw what Joseph Story had to say about an armed citizenry: "The militia is the natural defence of a free country against sudden foreign invasions, domestic insurrections, and domestic usurpations of power by rulers."[77]

By the way, when Story said "militia," he didn't mean only formally organized, state-sponsored military units. Those who drafted and ratified the Second Amendment didn't either. The gun-control crowd likes to claim that "militia" is basically equivalent to the

National Guard today. But no. Story wrote that when the Framers referred to "the security of a free state" in the text of the Second Amendment, they weren't talking about each state in the union, like Virginia or Pennsylvania or Connecticut. Instead, the Framers used the term *state* in what Story called "its most enlarged sense." It referred to "the people composing a particular nation or community."[78] Similarly, in deliberations on ratifying the Constitution, George Mason of Virginia said: "Who are the militia? They consist now of the whole people, except a few public officers."[79]

In other words, the Framers are talking about citizens, not professional soldiers. Like the Ukrainian citizens taking up arms and making Molotov cocktails.

Although the war isn't over at the time of this writing, and it has been a near-run thing so far, I'd say the Ukrainians have found arming citizens pretty useful in defending themselves against foreign invasions—wouldn't you?

The Supreme Court cited Joseph Story when, in *Heller*, it affirmed the individual right to keep and bear arms.[80] The Court did so again two years later when it ruled that the Second Amendment's individual right to keep and bear arms was such a fundamental right that it applied to states and municipalities. This was in the case *McDonald v. Chicago*. Justice Samuel Alito cited Story at length in his opinion. Here's the money line from Story that Justice Alito quoted: "The right of the citizens to keep and bear arms has justly been considered as the palladium of the liberties of a republic."[81]

Palladium isn't a word you hear too often today. It means "safeguard." So, Joseph Story was saying that, if you want to protect your liberties, the right to keep and bear arms is essential. Why is that? Because it "offers a strong moral check against the usurpation and arbitrary power of rulers." Story added that even if tyrants and invaders "are successful in the first instance," this right will "enable the people to resist and triumph over them."[82]

That's what the people of Ukraine hoped. Try telling them that the right to keep and bear arms is a relic.

Mistake #2: Restrictive Gun Laws

Ukraine's leaders failed to protect the right to armed self-defense in its constitution. So, it won't surprise you to learn that the country remained saddled with restrictive gun laws until the eve of the Russian invasion.

Now, some gun-control advocates might insist that Ukraine's gun laws weren't all that restrictive. They might even say that Ukraine had some of the more permissive gun laws in Europe.[83] But that's like being one of the tallest buildings in Topeka, Kansas.

Here are some examples of firearms restrictions under Ukraine's long-standing laws:[84]

- Ukrainian citizens couldn't own handguns.

- They had to be at least twenty-five to buy rifles and twenty-one to buy shotguns.
- Anyone looking to buy a gun had to submit to a background check. According to a special report from *Firearms News*, that check included "a mental exam, a fee for the gun license, a requirement for a gun safe as well as a permit showing that the safe is approved and installed." The report added that this process was supposed to take thirty days but "sometimes it takes several months."[85]

That's why a movement arose to enshrine a constitutional right to armed self-defense. But Ukraine never followed through. Big mistake.

Mistake #3: Ukraine Destroyed a Weapons Stockpile... with More Than a Little Help from Barack Obama

Ukraine made another critical mistake in 2005 and 2006. After the Soviet Union collapsed, Ukraine (like other former Soviet states) had a lot of weapons left over from that regime. That stockpile included not only artillery and anti-aircraft weapons but also small arms and ammunition. In fact, Ukraine's supply included four hundred thousand small arms, such as AK-47s, and more than fifteen thousand *tons* of ammunition.[86]

Those weapons would have come in handy in 2022. So, what happened?

DISARMED

What happened is that Ukraine destroyed its stockpile. And it did so with a young, anti-gun U.S. senator leading the charge. His name was Barack Obama.

In 2005, only months after being sworn in as a Democratic senator from Illinois, Obama went to Ukraine to view the weapon supplies. It was well known even then that Obama wanted to run for president. Here's what Senator Obama said when he saw all the arms and ammo: "We need to eliminate these stockpiles for the safety of the Ukrainian people and people around the world."[87]

Yes, that's what he said: "for the safety of the Ukrainian people."

Then Obama went home and landed $48 million in federal funding for Ukraine, which agreed to destroy all those weapons.

"For the safety of the Ukrainian people." How has that worked out?

Later, when Obama was president, he refused to arm Ukraine. The Obama administration kept refusing the Ukrainians' pleas for help even after Putin made his designs on Ukraine clear—even after Russia annexed Crimea, and even after the downing of Malaysia Airlines Flight 17. Ukraine had even appealed to the United States for radar-jamming and detection equipment to counter Russian anti-aircraft systems—the kind later used to shoot down Flight 17.[88]

As *National Review*'s Andrew McCarthy wrote in 2014, "We should be arming the Ukrainians not only because it is in our national interest to repel Putin's ambitions, but also because *we are the ones who disarmed the Ukrainians*" (emphasis in original).[89]

But Obama refused. *Sorry, no weapons for you, Ukraine.*

Eight years later, a new president—who happened to have been Obama's vice president, Joe Biden—had to scramble to rectify that mistake.

Yes, It *Can* Happen Here

Even if you care about the right to bear arms, you might look at Ukraine's mistakes and think: *So what? In the United States we already have the Second Amendment. Why do we need to worry about Ukraine's issues?*

That way of thinking is understandable.

But it misses the big picture.

Yes, the United States does have the Second Amendment, and most states have similar state constitutional analogues—thank goodness. But anti-gun forces undermine them at every turn.

You know Ukraine's prohibition on carrying guns outside the home? If you think that's bad—and it is—remember that powerful anti-gun forces in the United States push for similar restrictions. In fact, some states and localities nearly eliminated the right to carry outside the home. Then, in 2022, the U.S. Supreme Court issued a decision affirming that "bear arms" does indeed mean carry them outside the home. You don't need a governmental official to decide whether you can or can't enjoy that right, the Court declared.[90]

But even that unequivocal ruling hasn't stopped America's anti-gun forces. Less than a week after the Court handed down its decision, New York State threw a hissy fit against the Court's ruling by making it illegal to carry firearms in most public and private places.[91] New York openly defied the Supreme Court, since it was the state's previous carry law that the Court had struck down. New York governor Kathy Hochul proclaimed that New York was "just getting started" with restrictive gun laws and that she was "prepared to go back to muskets."[92] California and New Jersey soon passed sweeping new gun-carry prohibitions of their own.[93]

Also, only two days after the Supreme Court ruling, President Joe Biden signed the most restrictive federal gun-control law in nearly thirty years.[94]

The attacks on the Second Amendment are relentless.

Think back to the language that then-Senator Barack Obama used when discussing Ukraine's weapons supplies: "We need to eliminate these stockpiles for the safety of the Ukrainian people and people around the world."

Does that language sound familiar? It should. The anti-gun lobby in the United States constantly justifies its gun grabs in the name of "public safety."

It *can* happen here.

That's why it's so essential to protect the Second Amendment and broad gun rights, so we don't end up in the same desperate situation that Ukraine did.

3

TOO LITTLE, AND NEARLY TOO LATE: PAYING THE PRICE FOR FAILING TO PROTECT THE INDIVIDUAL RIGHT TO BEAR ARMS

There's another temptation when looking at Ukraine's experience. The temptation is to say, *Sure, Ukraine should have acted sooner, but didn't it eventually fix its gun laws and load up on weapons?*

Yes, Ukraine did change its gun laws and did receive arms from all over the world. But it's going too far to say the country "fixed" its laws, for reasons you'll see in this chapter.

Even more important, you need to think about timing. Ukraine's parliament, the Verkhovna Rada, passed the new law literally hours before Russia invaded. And Ukraine was so unprepared that it had to beg the world for small arms, ammunition, and other weaponry to confront Putin's forces.

To understand how much timing matters, consider this question: How would the situation have been different if the Ukrainian constitution had protected the people's right to keep and bear arms, and if nearly half of all households had had firearms, as in the United States?

One possibility is obvious. The Ukrainians—military and civilians—would have been prepared from the outset to mount a much stronger defense against the Russian invasion.

But there's another, less obvious possibility: *Russia might not have invaded at all.*

We're talking about deterrence. A well-armed population has a real deterrent effect, especially if civilians are living in a culture where lawful use of firearms is valued and they are well trained in using firearms. In 2019, analysts from the Modern War Institute at West Point highlighted lessons from Russia's 2014 invasion of Crimea. Their conclusion? "Learning from Ukraine's experience, other nations are taking proactive measures to improve their own defenses by arming civilian militias and volunteer reserve forces and…teach[ing] civilians how to fight like guerrillas."[95]

The Modern War Institute experts wrote this article three years *before* Russia's February 2022 invasion of Ukraine. It seems that Ukraine didn't learn enough from its own experience in 2014. Other countries did learn from Ukraine's experience, however, as we'll see in Chapter 5.

The key point here is that as important as is the right to own a gun, it's not sufficient either to deter a threat or to fend it off once the fighting begins. You also need enough people who are *proficient* in the use of guns.

In this chapter, you'll see how Ukrainians scrambled in early 2022 to buy firearms and get rudimentary training. It didn't have to be this way. Ukraine has suffered for its repeated failures to protect the people's gun rights and to ensure that a larger population is well trained in using firearms.

Everything Ukraine did up to the Russian invasion amounts to a sad case of too little, and almost too late.

This is a cautionary tale. Pay attention if you care about protecting the right to armed self-defense in the United States.

The good news is that Americans won't need to worry about scrambling to arm themselves the way Ukrainians did, because not only do we have the Second Amendment, we also have a longstanding private gun culture. The bad news is that forces all around us work tirelessly to take away the individual right to keep and bear arms. So, the lesson here is: never, ever let our governments, whether federal, state, or local, take away or infringe on our right to keep and bear arms.

Anti-Gunners Suddenly See the Light

You know the expression "There are no atheists in foxholes"? Well, now we have a corollary: "There are no anti-gunners when you're invaded by a foreign power."

Consider the about-face that Ukraine's leaders made.

It starts with President Volodymyr Zelenskyy. Up until the Russian invasion, he resisted efforts to loosen Ukraine's gun laws.[96] Do you recall the petition for a gun-rights constitutional amendment that gained tens of thousands of signatures in record time? Zelenskyy opposed it. Apparently, he thought that lifting some of Ukraine's firearms restrictions would be "premature."[97]

Fast-forward to February 2022. That's when Ukraine's parliament passed a law allowing Ukrainians to carry guns and act in self-defense.[98] The Rada (Ukraine's parliament) rushed through the bill two days after Putin ordered troops into eastern Ukraine. On the day he ordered troops into Ukraine, Putin appeared on Russian television to state: "I would like to emphasize again that Ukraine is not just a neighbouring country for us. It is an inalienable part of our own history, culture and spiritual space."[99] Russia's invasion began less than a day after the Rada approved the bill allowing the bearing of arms in Ukraine.[100]

Not only did President Zelenskyy sign the bill, as noted at the outset of this book, he also declared that the government "will give weapons to anyone who wants to defend the country."[101] Zelenskyy added, "The future of the Ukrainian people depends on every Ukrainian."[102] Not just on soldiers. On *every Ukrainian*. In America, we might refer to "every citizen" as "the people," as in the "right of the people to keep and bear arms."

The president proved true to his word. Within days, Ukraine's government had handed out more than twenty-five thousand automatic rifles and about ten million rounds of ammunition, plus rocket-propelled grenades and launchers—all to civilians.[103]

Other Ukrainian leaders joined the chorus. The nation's defense ministry called on Ukrainians to make Molotov cocktails to "neutralize the occupier."[104] Radio stations issued bulletins explaining how to make those incendiary weapons.[105]

Suddenly Ukrainians were talking about following America's example. Ukraine's former minister of infrastructure said that his people had come to "understand you should fight back." He explained that "we have become a lot more American in this way." A Ukrainian lawyer told a reporter, "We always look at the Second Amendment of the U.S. Constitution."[106]

If only they had followed the American example years earlier, when they had the chance.

Eight Years Too Late

Although Ukraine's leaders did everything they could to gear up quickly, they knew they hadn't prepared properly. Zelenskyy repeatedly begged the world for guns, ammunition, and other weaponry.[107] He found himself in this position because, as we've seen, Ukraine had destroyed its Cold War stockpile of weapons and ammo with an assist from President Obama. Later, President Obama refused Ukraine's requests for arms.

Finally, eight years after President Obama turned down those requests, President Biden answered Zelenskyy's call for help.[108] On announcing one of many security packages, Biden said how important it was to "provide Ukraine with weapons and equipment to defend itself."[109]

Here you saw another sign that there are no gun skeptics when an invasion happens. Biden stands as one of the most anti-gun politicians in U.S. history. As a Democratic senator from Delaware, he helped to push through the 1994 Federal Assault Weapons Ban, which banned many ordinary semiautomatic rifles and standard capacity magazines.[110] And as president, he signed the most restrictive gun law since he had orchestrated that sweeping legislation.[111]

Plenty of other vocal opponents of gun rights eagerly endorsed arming Ukrainian civilians. For example, on February 24, the day of Russia's invasion, the left-wing grassroots political organization Occupy Democrats sent out this tweet: "BREAKING: Ukraine's Interior Minister announces that 10,000 automatic rifles have been handed out to the civilians of Kyiv as they prepare to fight tooth and nail to defend their homes against Putin's invasion. RT [retweet] IF YOU STAND WITH THE BRAVE UKRAINIAN PEOPLE!"[112]

So, Occupy Democrats cheered arming civilians with automatic rifles? That's interesting, because less than five months later, the progressive group tweeted out the following: "BREAKING: If you support an assault weapons ban and are thrilled that President Biden announced that he is 'determined' to ban 'weapons of war' like assault weapons and he is 'not going to stop' until they are outlawed like they were in 1994, please retweet and follow us!"[113]

Let's get this straight. Anti-gun groups like Occupy Democrats want the U.S. government to ban Americans from owning *semiautomatic* firearms, which are ordinary civilian firearms that gun-controllers misleadingly call "assault weapons" and "weapons of war." Law-abiding Americans have commonly owned semiautomatic firearms for well over a century, using them for such peaceable activities as hunting, target practice, and self-defense. But American anti-gunners celebrate when another government gives its citizens thousands of *automatic* weapons, which (unlike semiautomatics) are actual military weapons. Automatic weapons—also known as machine guns—can achieve extraordinarily high rates of fire with the shooter merely holding down the trigger. By contrast, semiautomatic guns limit the rate of fire because they require a discrete trigger pull to fire every round. This fundamental difference between automatic weapons (machine guns) and semiautomatic firearms has not been lost on the U.S. Supreme Court, which recognized the clear differences in their *Staples v. United States* decision back in 1994.[114]

Why do Biden and other leftists support arming Ukrainians while trying to disarm Americans? Simple—because the left is the party of all-powerful government. As described in Chapter 5, authoritarian governments or wannabe tyrants always try to disarm the people, so that the people cannot resist their power. The Ukrainian people pose no threat or deterrent to those who seek more and more unchecked power in this country, but free, independent, armed Americans do.

Also, there are people among U.S. elites who favor America's enemies and want to see this country weakened militarily. It is to China's potential advantage, for example, for money and military aid to be siphoned off to Ukraine, rather than being spent to prepare for a possible conflict with that country. In less than a year after the commencement of the Ukraine war, the U.S. has provided approximately $100 billion in strategic aid to Ukraine.[115] In 2022, the Marines shipped nearly a quarter of its M777 Howitzer systems to Ukraine.[116] By early April 2022, just a month and a half into the war, the U.S. had given seven thousand Javelin anti-tank missiles to Ukraine, about a third of our inventory.[117] It will take about three to four years to replace just those seven thousand missiles, and longer to replace those and any shipped since that time.[118] By that same time early in the war, the U.S. had provided two thousand Stinger anti-aircraft missiles to Ukraine, about a quarter of our inventory. Up until then, the U.S. had not procured any Stinger missiles since 2003.[119]

According to the Wall Street Journal, "It is difficult to determine exactly how many pieces of equipment the U.S. has sent or promised, in part because of the sheer scale: more than 10,000 antiaircraft systems and antiarmor systems, more than 200 helicopters and tanks, and more than 1.5 million artillery and ammunition rounds are among the gear the U.S. has committed."[120] Included in these are 155mm mobile howitzers, Javelin and Stinger portable rockets, Himars (High Mobility Artillery Rocket System), Bradley Fighting Vehicles and M1A2 Abrams tanks. The State Department has reported that from the invasion of Ukraine in February 2022 to the time of this writing in March 2023, the United States alone has spent $32.2 billion on security assistance.[121] This does not even include the considerable spending of NATO allies, like Germany, France, and the United Kingdom.[122] But security assistance isn't everything needed to support the defense of an ill-prepared people. According to research by the Council on Foreign Relations, the United States spent a whopping $76.8 billion in aid to Ukraine—$3.9 billion in humanitarian aid, $26.4 billion in financial aid, and $46.6 billion in net military assistance.[123] This assistance includes thousands upon thousands of small arms and large amounts of ammunition, which Ukraine could have had on hand had it permitted a trained, armed citizenry. But it didn't. Rather than Ukraine learning from the mistakes of others, it appears that the U.S. is paying for the mistakes of Ukraine.

One U.S. military analyst noted concerns expressed by the Pentagon itself:

> Bill LaPlante, undersecretary of defense for acquisition and sustainment, explained that the big lesson of U.S. material support for Ukraine is that "production matters." By supplying weapon systems to Ukraine, we have depleted our own stockpiles of weapons, such as the

High Mobility Artillery Rocket System (HIMARS) and air-defense systems. Production of these critical systems lags. This has created problems for the United States, especially in the Indo-Pacific region, where we face our primary strategic challenge from China.[124]

If I were China, I'd be licking my lips every time America poured more billions of defense money and materiel into Ukraine. It's not that the U.S. is wrong to support Ukraine, but it can put this country at a strategic disadvantage regarding our main adversary. For some people, that's not a bug but a feature.

Don't let the "we stand with Ukraine" rhetoric fool you. Gun-prohibitionist forces in the United States are pushing and will continue to push to deprive you of your Second Amendment rights. And as Ukraine has learned the hard way, gutting the right to keep and bear arms leaves you dangerously unprepared to defend yourself, your family, your community, and even your country.

The Gun-Control Measures You Didn't Hear About

Once the Russian invasion began, Ukraine relaxed its gun laws and handed out tens of thousands of weapons to civilians. That should be a victory for supporters of the right to keep and bear arms, right?

Well, it's better than nothing. But when you look at the full picture, you see many shortcomings and missed opportunities.

Start with the new gun law itself. Yes, it allowed the citizens of Ukraine to carry arms and defend their country. That's good. But even with the future of the nation at stake, Ukraine's politicians couldn't shift out of their gun-control mindset completely.

The Ukrainian parliament imposed severe limits that drew little attention in the Western press. Specifically, the Rada loosened gun restrictions solely as an emergency measure, so that the people would enjoy the right to carry only as long as the war with Russia lasted. And civilians could use their firearms *only* to repel Russian forces.[125]

What about all those guns that Ukraine's government handed out to civilians? The law stipulated that citizens would need to turn in the firearms and unused ammo to the national police "no later than 10 days" after war's end.[126]

In fact, less than two months into the war, Ukraine's Ministry of Defense ordered various volunteer units in the Territorial Defense Forces to turn in their weapons for "storage" purposes. In the order, the commander of the Territorial Defense Forces wrote:

> *You and I have been defending our country side by side for almost two months now.... You, the volunteers, have already provided real help to the Armed Forces by releasing combat units to carry out combat missions. With weapons in your hands, you liberated the north of Ukraine from the Russian invaders, and now you are fighting for the south and east of Ukraine. The Armed Forces and your communities greatly appreciate your*

bravery and dedication. Some of our regions have been liberated from the occupiers and no hostilities are taking place there.... That is why in these regions it is time to concentrate weapons in designated storage areas.... We will keep the powder dry.[127]

After the war had been going on for a year, these orders were expanded to more and more civilians. Governor Serhii Lysak in the Dnipropetrovsk Oblast has now ordered that civilians who received weapons at the outset of the war must return them. "Civilians must return their firearms and ammunition within 10 days," Lysak stated in a messaging app on March 6, 2023, during a meeting with law enforcement officers in his region.[128] Lysak's order follows an earlier "decree issued by Ukraine's interior minister on March 7, 2022, titled, 'Ensuring the Participation of Civilians in the Protection of Ukraine.' The decree states that civilians must return their issued weapons within 10 days after the cancellation, or termination, of martial law."[129] In other words: *Thanks for everything. But no more guns for you.*

It gets worse. The Rada used the new gun laws to reinforce the Unified State Register of Civilian Firearms—that is, the national gun registry.[130] In case you don't know, gun registries are very dangerous because they prepare the way for confiscation. That's exactly how communist dictator Nicolae Ceaușescu used gun-registration lists in Romania, for example.[131] Current federal law prohibits the U.S. government from keeping such records.[132]

DISARMED

Even if registry information is not misused by the government that collected it, the information may fall into the wrong hands and put gun owners at risk. Second Amendment historian and scholar Stephen Halbrook has revealed how the Nazis, when they seized power in 1933, exploited Germany's gun registry to identify and disarm Jews and other political opponents. Then, in 1938, the Third Reich ordered all Jews to surrender their guns or spend twenty years in a concentration camp. So, the Nazis had rendered Jews defenseless by the time they launched their infamous Kristallnacht attacks.[133]

The Nazis followed a similar playbook when they occupied France in 1940. Halbrook explains: "Nazi military officials posted notices that all who failed to turn in their firearms within 24 hours would be executed. French police had gun registration records, making it convenient for the Germans to find the 'legal' gun owners."[134]

The French example highlights how invading forces can exploit gun registries. Did the Ukrainians learn nothing from history? Wouldn't it help Putin to have his soldiers track down Ukrainian gun owners and confiscate their weapons, imprison them, or even kill them?

In fact, soon before the invasion began, a leaked letter revealed that the United States had alerted the United Nations to credible information indicating that "Russian forces are creating lists of identified Ukrainians to be killed or sent to camps following a military occupation."[135] Several weeks into the war, *The Guardian* of London published a first-person account describing life in a city in eastern

Ukraine that the Russians had occupied. The Ukrainian correspondent wrote:

> [My father's] house is now surrounded by trenches and destroyed houses and his new neighbours are Russian soldiers. They have prepared a list of individuals to "hunt," people who may own a gun, are rich or "dangerous," including businessmen, activists, military and their families. My father observed one hunt for a local businessman, who had already escaped when the raiding party arrived.[136]

Oh, and the Rada even spelled out the concept of "weapon-free zones" in Ukraine.[137] You may know from our experience in the United States that a "gun-free zone" sign might as well say, "Come and get us—we're sitting ducks." It's an invitation to violent criminals.

It's no accident, for example, that 94 percent of mass public shootings between 1950 and 2019 occurred in "gun-free zones," according to a study by the Crime Prevention Research Center.[138] It's also no accident that anti-gun New York defied the Supreme Court by effectively declaring large swaths of the state to be gun-free zones.[139]

The Ukrainian parliament imposed a final gun-control measure by regulating the temporary import and export of civilian firearms and ammunition.[140] So, right as Ukrainians confronted an existential threat and their president was calling on citizens to take up arms, the Rada made it harder for those citizens to find arms.

DISARMED

A lack of guns and ammunition ended up handicapping the Ukrainians on many occasions. Six months into the war, a top adviser to Ukraine's president told NBC News that the Ukrainians desperately needed ammo because Russia "was firing up to 60,000 rounds of ammunition per day, forcing Ukraine to respond in turn."[141] A month later, *The New York Times* reported, "The Russians have much more ammunition than the Ukrainians and pound their forces every day." The commander of a volunteer unit (again, these are civilians, not professional soldiers) said that the Ukrainians were suffering "great losses" because "we don't have ammunition."[142]

Examining Ukraine's various gun-control measures, one American analyst noted, "Ukraine is determined to join the European Union and therefore does not wish to contravene EU laws, one of which mandates licensing for most semi-automatic firearms."[143] It's hard to believe that with Russian forces storming their homeland, Ukrainian politicians were thinking about how to maintain gun control when all this blew over. If Ukraine didn't defend itself successfully, they wouldn't have a country at all.

Unprepared

Another problem with Ukraine's new gun laws is the obvious one: the timing. Again, the Rada gave Ukraine's more than forty million citizens less than a day's notice that they would finally enjoy the privilege (which should be a *right*) to defend themselves, their loved ones, and their country with firearms.

Putin's actions in Crimea starting in 2014, and his massing of troops along Ukraine's border as early as April 2021—almost a year before he launched the invasion—did prompt the Ukrainian government to make some changes. For example, in 2021 the government recognized the volunteer Territorial Defense Forces as an official part of national defense.[144] But even as Ukraine's leaders acknowledged citizen resistance as essential to defending the nation, they didn't give citizens free access to firearms.

Remember, to secure your community or country, you need enough citizens who know how to use a gun safely, responsibly, and effectively. Ukraine's leaders didn't do enough to make that happen. They neither protected the right to bear arms nor encouraged a private gun culture.

How do we know Ukraine took action too late? The lack of preparedness became clear even before Russia invaded.

As noted in Chapter 1, a military historian and expert on guerrilla warfare called out Ukraine's inaction more than two months before the invasion. He observed, "Ukrainians are already talking about waging guerrilla warfare if the Russians invade." He also noted that a Ukrainian military official had floated the idea of arming the Ukrainian people. "Those are potent threats," the historian wrote. "But why wait for a Russian invasion to make these preparations? The Ukrainian government needs to start distributing weapons now and, with the help of U.S. and other Western military advisers, training personnel to carry out guerrilla warfare."¹⁴⁵

You might applaud the Ukraine government's decision to recognize the Territorial Defense Forces in a 2021 law. The problem is that the militias didn't come together until the beginning of 2022—only weeks before the invasion.¹⁴⁶ And the government didn't do much to supply these volunteers with firearms. In fact, even professional soldiers frequently needed to rely on equipment donated by volunteers.¹⁴⁷ Members of the Territorial Defense Forces had to bring their own guns—if they had access to any.

One Ukrainian volunteer, a former taxi driver, summed up the matter perfectly. As he shopped at army surplus shops for supplies to take back to the front lines, he pointed out: "Ukraine wasn't ready for this war.… Therefore, not everyone has everything."¹⁴⁸

President Zelenskyy revealed how desperate Ukraine was for help when he put out an open call for foreign volunteers with combat experience. He even announced a separate unit of the Territorial Defense Forces for foreigners: the International Brigade.¹⁴⁹ Zelenskyy said, "Anyone who wants to join the defence of security in Europe and the world can come and stand side by side with the Ukrainians against the invaders of the 21st century."¹⁵⁰

It's not as if Ukraine had a shortage of civilians willing and able to defend their country. A poll by the Kyiv International Institute of Sociology in December 2021 showed that a third of Ukrainians were ready to take up arms to defend their country. Another 21.7 percent were ready to go even further by joining a civil resistance movement.[151] That's more than half the country willing to participate in armed defense.

Two months after the invasion, another survey asked citizens, "Would you be prepared to take up arms to defend Ukraine?" More than 70 percent answered positively, including 4.2 percent who said they had already done so and another 35.8 percent who said they were "completely prepared" to do so.[152]

Ukrainians showed how ready they were by racing out to buy guns as soon as the Rada gave them permission to carry firearms. Gun stores saw record-breaking sales, with customers enduring long lines to buy weapons. Stores sold out of AR-15s—rifles that anti-gunners want to ban in the United States. Ukrainian police reported that they registered ten thousand new guns in the first few weeks of February alone.[153] Given that many Ukrainians ignored the gun-registration requirements, the actual number of weapons likely rose much higher. (Stephen Halbrook reports: "As late as 2018, there were 892,854 registered firearms in Ukraine, compared to an estimated 3.5 million 'illegal' firearms. This is the same pattern in states like California and New York, where laws requiring the registration of so-called 'assault weapons' are largely ignored.")[154]

Ukrainians understood the need for firearms training too. On the eve of the invasion, *The New York Post* reported, "Tens of thousands of ordinary people across the Eastern European nation are learning to handle weapons."[155] One surgeon turned to his twenty-three-year-old daughter to learn how to shoot.[156] A fifty-two-year-old marketing researcher and mother of three armed herself with a Zbroyar Z-15 carbine. To learn how to handle it, she attended a two-week sniper's course.[157] To be fair, Ukraine didn't lack training altogether before the invasion. Military youth organizations brought some young people to shooting ranges, for example. But to be robustly prepared for armed defense, training opportunities need to be more extensive. Those opportunities mushroomed once war began. In March, for instance, the city of Ivano-Frankivsk opened its five shooting ranges, which military youth groups had previously used, for civilian training.[158] In Lviv, a youth center began running summer classes for high school students in weapons handling, shooting, and basic self-defense.[159] In a nearby suburb, volunteers asked a local principal if they could use classrooms to teach adults how to handle guns. They trained about a thousand people in the first month. One volunteer explained, "The army doesn't have the capacity to train everyone, so we set this school up to help."[160]

Volunteers helped in many other ways. In Odesa, a twenty-six-year-old woman named Anna Bondarenko founded the private Ukrainian Volunteer Service (UVS). Six months after the war began, *The Atlantic* reported:

> UVS has fielded thousands of requests, creating a set of websites, chat sites, and chatbots that eventually matched more than 100,000 people—accountants,

drivers, medics—with more than 900 organizations across the country. Ukrainians find UVS via Instagram, Facebook, Telegram, TikTok; when you type I want to volunteer into a Ukrainian Google search, UVS is the first organization to come up. Bondarenko's team has sent volunteers to help distribute food packages to people who lost their homes, clean up rubble after bombing raids, and, for those willing to take real risks, to drive cars or buses into war zones and pull people out. People wrote to them for advice: How should we make Molotov cocktails? How should we evacuate? And the volunteers tried to find experts who could give them answers.[161]

Ultimately, as many as five hundred thousand volunteers and reservists joined the battle. That came as part of a "general mobilization" of the Ukrainian public that Zelenskyy ordered after the invasion and that the Rada later extended. For context, Ukraine had about two hundred thousand active-duty troops when the war began.[162] Hundreds of thousands of Ukrainians living abroad even returned home to join the cause.[163]

Many of these brave people lamented their lack of preparation. Right after the invasion, a thirty-three-year-old construction worker who had been living in France raced home to report for duty. A *New Yorker* reporter sat next to him on the bus ride across Europe. The reporter later recounted that the man "neither ate nor slept, and his anxiety seemed to increase as we neared Ukraine." The *New Yorker* account continues: "He had never fired a weapon. 'I don't know where they're going to send me,' he told us midway through Poland, his hands trembling. 'I don't know what's going to happen to me.' Embarrassed by the tears welling in his eyes, he explained, 'Not everyone is ready for this.'"[164]

Deadly Mistake

In confronting the Russian assault, Ukraine could count on one major blessing at least: a population of patriots willing to sacrifice their lives in armed defense of their country.

But its politicians failed to leverage this great attribute, and they failed to protect those patriots. For too long they dismissed the importance of the right to keep and bear arms. It's great that the chair of Ukraine's parliament extolled "the sacred right to self-defense" in February 2022.[165] But Ukrainian leaders could have and should have done so weeks, months, or years earlier. And even at that moment of existential crisis, Ukraine's leaders retained major elements of a gun-control regime.

So, Ukraine for decades restricted gun rights and then only belatedly (and incompletely) attempted to fix the problem. A growing contingent of powerful figures in the United States wants to move in the opposite direction: to go from a nation that stands for the private right to keep and bear arms to become yet another country that robs its citizens of the right to self-defense.

To understand Ukraine's story is to understand what a deadly mistake that would be.

Now, some anti-gunners would argue that focusing on Ukraine's mistakes on guns and gun rights ignores the fact that Russia is a nuclear-armed country with one of the world's most powerful militaries. They ask, *What are civilians with rifles really going to do to stop a military juggernaut?*

But this assessment not only overlooks what happened in the first several months of the war, when seemingly overmatched Ukraine surprised military experts with its successes at every turn. It also overlooks history—including very recent history—which shows that small arms are essential for national defense, even in an age of missiles, drones, and nukes.

We'll take up that history in the next chapter.

4

YES, SMALL ARMS MATTER—A LOT

> *We are like a hive of bees. One bee is nothing, but a thousand can defeat a big force.*
> —Yaroslav Honchar, head of a volunteer Ukrainian attack-drone crew, quoted in *The Wall Street Journal*, September 20, 2022

Like many other gun prohibitionists, President Joe Biden mocks the idea that the right to keep and bear arms is a last resort against tyranny.

As we saw in Chapter 1, Biden has dismissed "those brave right-wing Americans who say [the Second Amendment is] all about keeping America independent and safe, if you want to fight against the country, you need an F-15 [fighter jet]. You need something more than a gun."[166]

Biden made that statement in a speech on August 30, 2022. But he says stuff like this a lot. Three months earlier, for example, he went on an anti-gun tirade while speaking to reporters at the White House. The president scoffed at people who say, "You have to be able to take on the government when they're wrong." If you really want to take on the government, Biden claimed, "You need an F-15, you know? Or you need an Abrams tank."[167] In 2021, President Biden insisted, "You need F-15s and maybe some nuclear weapons."[168] During the 2020 presidential campaign, Biden said, "If you're going to take on the government you need an F-15 with Hellfire missiles."[169]

You get the idea.

No matter how many times Biden repeats this argument, though, it's still not true.

For starters, it contradicts a central claim that Biden and other anti-gunners make: that semiautomatic firearms are "weapons of war" that have no place in civilian life. As Heritage Foundation legal fellow Amy Swearer aptly put it, a semiautomatic rifle like the AR-15 is either "a useless hunk of carbon fiber without any value in a hypothetical armed defense against a tyrant's military forces, or it is a war zone weapon that should be limited to the battlefield. It cannot be both at the same time."[170]

At best, Biden's F-15 line is a straw man argument. No one seriously suggests that unorganized civilians possessing only small arms can *alone* defeat a powerful modern military force. Second Amendment supporters don't see armed resistance as a fantasy out of the movie *Red Dawn*. The point is that small arms form an essential *component* of a good defense against either a tyrannical government at home or a foreign invader. One of the advantages of small arms, as we'll see, is that they help to get your hands on bigger weapons. And if armed citizens contribute to an effective resistance, they are more likely to attract strong outside support. Or, even if a tyrannical power overruns an area, having the ability to fight back and make that occupation costly and difficult can help to drive the invaders from that area.

Again, just ask Ukraine whether an armed citizenry matters. President Volodymyr Zelenskyy confronted a nuclear-armed country that had the world's second most powerful military.[171] Did he follow the Biden line and say, *Well, we don't have nuclear weapons, so I guess we should give up?*

No, of course not. He handed out all those rifles to civilians. Zelenskyy recognized that armed citizens represent an important line of defense.

In the first several months of the war with Russia, Ukraine shocked military experts again and again. Why? Yes, Ukraine had a small air force. Yes, the United States and other nations sent long-range rockets, anti-tank weapons, and artillery.[172] But small arms proved crucial throughout the fight.

And, it's not as if Ukraine stands as an exception. History is replete with examples of outmanned, outgunned forces resisting and even defeating much more powerful militaries. The renowned law professor Sanford Levinson, a self-proclaimed liberal,[173] summed up the lessons from history when he said it is "simply silly" to claim that "small arms are irrelevant against nuclear armed states." Think of the decades Great Britain spent embroiled in "The Troubles" with Northern Ireland. Britain's advanced weaponry "proved almost totally beside the point," Levinson wrote.[174]

The historical record also shows that the more a population is *trained* to use firearms, the better its chances will be to resist tyrannical forces.

David versus Goliath

Let's start with an obvious point: Russia has a vastly more powerful military than does Ukraine.

Here are some basic facts that illustrate the gulf that separated Russia and Ukraine when the war began:[175]

- In 2021, Russia spent nearly ten times as much on its armed forces as Ukraine did.
- Russia had five times the active personnel.
- Russia had far more air power, including ten times the number of airplanes and fifteen times the number of helicopters. A month into the war, *The New York Times* reported, "Russia is believed to fly some 200 sorties per day while Ukraine flies five to 10."[176]
- Russia had nearly five times the number of tanks and other armored fighting vehicles.

- The huge gap in defense spending showed up in the kinds of weapons each side used. Early in the war, Ukraine relied on old weaponry, mostly from the Soviet era.[177] Videos showed Ukrainian forces armed with rifles that dated to before World War II and machine guns designed before World War I.[178]

So, you can see why, when the war began, CNN ran the headline "Ukraine and Russia's Militaries Are David and Goliath."[179]

Of course, in the Bible, David defeats Goliath.

Hitting Goliath with Small Arms

From the beginning, small arms played a crucial role in Ukraine's defense against Russia. Most press coverage of foreign military aid to Ukraine focused on missiles, tanks, and the like. But guns and ammunition made up a big piece of the aid. For example, by September 2022, the United States had sent the Ukrainians more than ten thousand small arms (rifles, pistols, shotguns, machine guns, and grenade launchers) and about sixty million rounds of ammunition.[180] Meanwhile, American arms makers donated thousands of rifles to Ukraine, sold others at a discount, and supplied parts for the Ukrainians to make their own small arms.[181] What's the point of all these small arms in the hands of Ukrainians against Russia, which is a nuclear power?

An expert in the arms trade explained why guns and ammo prove so useful: "Without them, Ukrainian soldiers—and the civilians who have joined them—cannot defend themselves. This equipment is also simple to learn how to use, and relatively small and lightweight, making it easy to ship large amounts from one country to another."[182] Easier than F-15s, certainly.

About a month into the Russia-Ukraine war, a leading site dedicated to firearms news called the AK-74 rifle "by far the most ubiquitous weapon" in the conflict.[183] When Ukraine's leaders put out a worldwide call for military aid, they specifically asked for rifles (including sniper rifles), pistols, ammunition, and ammunition magazines.[184] So Ukrainians, military and civilians, have used pistols, revolvers, shotguns, bolt-action rifles, semiautomatic rifles—you name it.[185]

At the war's six-month mark, NBC News revealed how vital small arms remained to Ukraine's efforts. NBC noted that although Ukraine's pleas "for fighter jets, air defense systems and long-range weapons" drew the most attention, the country was "burning through its stores of necessities that most modern militaries take for granted." Those necessities included things like food, boots, and first-aid kits but also "small arms and ammunition."[186]

Ukraine made good use of its small arms. Only days into the fighting, a Ukrainian sniper killed a high-ranking Russian general, Andrei Sukhovetsky.[187] Soon *The Washington Post* reported that Ukrainians were killing opposing generals "at a rate not seen since

DISARMED

World War II."[188] David Petraeus, the retired four-star general who served as commander of the U.S. Central Command, told CNN that Ukrainian snipers "have just been picking them off left and right."[189] By June, Ukraine's Defense Ministry reported that its forces had killed a dozen Russian generals.[190] The number "astonished military analysts," according to *The New York Times*.[191] As General Petraeus noted, it is "very, very uncommon" for generals to be killed in action.[192]

Generals weren't the only target for Ukrainian snipers. In June, credible reports emerged to show that a Ukrainian sniper had killed "The Executioner," a notorious Russian mercenary who had reportedly killed civilians and prisoners of war.[193] Around the same time, *The Times* of London reported that a volunteer unit of Ukrainian snipers had taken out three hundred Russian troops since the start of the war.[194] And Zenger News posted multiple videos that appeared to show snipers wiping out groups of Russian soldiers.[195]

Not bad for a supposedly overmatched military force—fighting against a nuclear power with an air force consisting of fighter jets similar to F-15s. Someone better wake up Joe Biden and let him know about this!

MARK W. SMITH

How Civilians Are Difference Makers

Those Ukrainian successes weren't flukes. As the war progressed, military analysts around the world sounded the same theme: *Boy, I didn't think Ukraine could stand up to Russia like this.*[196]

Vladimir Putin expected his troops to march right into Ukraine's capital city, Kyiv. Most experts figured Putin was right. "When the invasion began, almost everyone thought Kyiv would fall in days," remembered political scientist Daniel Treisman.[197] As we've seen, the chairman of the Joint Chiefs of Staff, General Mark Milley, reportedly told U.S. officials that the Russians could take Kyiv within seventy-two hours.[198]

Except it didn't happen. Ukraine repelled the advance on Kyiv. The Associated Press called Russia's failure to take the capital "a defeat for the ages."[199]

During the assault on Kyiv, the Russians sent elite airborne troops to capture an airport northwest of the city. They planned to use the airport to bring in eighteen transport aircraft, making it the staging ground for the final assault on the capital. The Ukrainians didn't have advanced weaponry. They mainly had rifles, some anti-aircraft guns, and a few shoulder-fired missiles. The Russians, meanwhile, had dozens of helicopters armed with missiles. "It was like turning up with a knife to a gunfight," a Ukrainian lieutenant later said.[200] Still, the Ukrainians held off the Russians.

Or what about Ukraine's lightning offensive in September that forced Russian troops in eastern Ukraine to retreat? Nobody saw that coming—least of all the Russians.[201]

Why did Ukraine keep defying the experts' expectations? This book isn't meant to offer an extended military analysis of the war in Ukraine. Plenty of analysts are exploring the strategies, tactics, and weaponry used on both sides. And obviously many factors came into play that have allowed Ukraine to achieve surprising successes.

But I want to call attention to a broader point that too often gets lost amid discussions of long-range artillery, logistics, Russian blunders, and the like. The point is this: civilians—especially motivated civilians carrying small arms—played a vital role in the Ukrainian war effort from the beginning. Ukraine's top military commander, General Valeriy Zaluzhny, made the point picturesquely in describing the defense of Kyiv in the first weeks of the invasion: "Military theory does not account for regular dudes with track pants and hunting rifles."[202]

This is a crucial lesson for America and the West (as well as for invaders and would-be oppressors).

Take this assessment from an experienced writer on international security and military history, Sébastien Roblin. He asked why "Ukraine has been an immense success story," unlike the long and costly U.S. wars in Vietnam, Afghanistan, and Iraq. The first reason Roblin gave was: "Ukrainian society as a whole was willing to fight in defense of its country. The government wasn't reliant on the U.S. military to prop it up and to cajole reluctant recruits to defend it."²⁰³

Here you see another example of why Joe Biden and other anti-gun crusaders are dead wrong when they suggest that civilians are helpless in the face of a mighty military power. Civilians can be the make-or-break factor. Remember, Ukraine had only two hundred thousand active-duty troops when Russia invaded, but a half million volunteers came in alongside them, including expatriates who rushed home to the front.

Those who chalked up Ukraine's surprising successes to foreign military aid missed some key factors. Yes, military aid makes a difference. (Or to use Joe Biden's terms, yes, F-15s help.) But pouring lots of money into high-tech weapons doesn't guarantee success. Russia found that out the hard way in Ukraine. So did the United States in Vietnam, Afghanistan, and Iraq. The effectiveness and commitment of armed citizens make a huge difference as to whether insurgencies will leverage foreign support. Roblin wrote: "Ukraine's spirit of national resistance has also meant that most of the U.S. arms transferred to local forces have been used for their intended purpose. In contrast, corruption and disloyalty (and ineptness) saw huge quantities of U.S. military aid to Afghanistan, Iraq and South Vietnam go missing and even end up with enemy forces."²⁰⁴

Another overlooked factor is that armed citizens can help *attract* foreign support. Ukraine's many surprising successes against Russia undoubtedly kept foreign aid flowing. Other countries, the United

States especially, saw that they were supporting an effective military force. And throughout history, the most effective citizens' wars have tended to be those that attract outside support in the form of arms, supplies, and even soldiers.[205] For example, during the Revolutionary War, some successes against the British helped Americans attract aid from France, without which the American Revolution probably would have failed.[206] By contrast, during the American Civil War, the Confederacy lost a good opportunity to secure recognition from Britain and France when the Union repelled the Confederate invasion at Antietam. The South's defeats at Gettysburg and Vicksburg the next year essentially killed all chances for recognition.[207]

Ukraine's "spirit of national resistance" extended well beyond the hundreds of thousands of militia members and other volunteers who formally took up arms. A big reason Ukraine held Kyiv and other major cities early in the war had to do with the civilians who supported the uniformed troops and helped stymie the Russian advance. In Kyiv, civilians "dropped everything to protect the city," according to *The New Yorker*.[208] An NBC News reporter on the ground said: "In the cities under siege, brave Ukrainians aren't just the ones wearing uniforms. Volunteer fighters, civilians armed with assault rifles, [patrol] central Kyiv, ready to defend their country and protect their families."[209]

The New York Times reported: "Vans and cars with armed men without uniforms careened along the streets. Checkpoints went up seemingly at every stoplight, with men and women in civilian clothes, carrying rifles, stopping cars."[210]

The Wall Street Journal described other examples of Ukrainians who "found the will and means to resist" Putin's forces:

> *They formed armed groups with whatever weapons they could lay their hands on. They fed and equipped fighters and billeted them in their homes. They shimmied up trees in search of cellphone reception to report on enemy movements. The result looked like something little seen in modern warfare—a domestic insurgency fused onto a traditional army.*[211]

That domestic insurgency included Ukrainians who wore jeans and no body armor. They brandished "a grab bag of weapons, including pump-action shotguns and a handful of rocket-propelled grenades." Describing one makeshift unit, the *Journal* reported, "Around half of their number, which included a psychotherapist, a firefighter and a bus driver, had never fought before."[212] In the city of Irpin, outside Kyiv, the mayor, city councilors, and utility workers joined in with AK-47s to fire on Russian armored vehicles.[213]

Time magazine wrote of "unarmed civilians blocking the roads and lying on the ground in front of Russian tanks; girls throwing Molotov cocktails at Russian military vehicles from car windows; and even women hitting enemy drones with jars of pickled tomatoes."[214]

People around the world watched videos showing ordinary Ukrainians resisting the Russians. In one viral video, a woman told a Russian soldier, "Take these seeds so sunflowers grow when you die here." In another, an old couple chased three armed Russian soldiers from their property.[215]

Ukrainians parked bulldozers and cement mixers in the middle of roads to block Russia's armored column. On the outskirts of Kyiv, some Ukrainians had scrawled a message on the vehicles for the Russian invaders: "Welcome to hell."[216]

They certainly made life hell for the Russians, who withdrew from Kyiv.

The leader of a Ukrainian special-forces unit reflected on the importance of civilian engagement: "I don't think one person or another can say they stopped the assault on Kyiv. Everyone did."[217]

You Can Do a Lot with Small Arms

Three days into Russia's assault on Kyiv, *The New York Times* reported that Ukrainians had "defied expectations by slowing and in some cases halting the Russian army's advance." But the *Times* expressed doubts that Ukraine could keep it up: "It's unclear how civilians with assault rifles might stop artillery from bombarding the city or Russian tanks from rolling into the streets."[218]

That statement reflected the conventional wisdom of the time— the same "wisdom" and apparent historical ignorance that still leads

Joe Biden and other gun prohibitionists to scoff at the idea of civilian resistance.

But in truth, this kind of urban warfare is tailor-made for small arms.

Ukrainian cities from Kyiv to Severodonetsk to Mariupol became the scenes of street fighting, even hand-to-hand combat.[219] At that point, advantages in missiles, air power, and the rest tend to melt away. Writing in the *Los Angeles Times*, three experts on modern warfare summed up the matter this way:

> *Urban warfare reduces all the strengths of the attacker, even if it is a superior military force. The attackers lack situational awareness to see into dense terrain with full clarity. They are confined to narrow streets and alleys, and are prevented from spreading out to support each other.*
>
> *Concrete obstacles and buildings provide the defense with protection and concealment. The attacking military must crisscross open areas and exposed streets to attack a defender behind walls of concrete. The attackers will have no clue where the enemy is amid the thousands of potential hiding spots.*[220]

An invading force has tanks, sure. But as an analysis from the Modern War Institute at West Point put it, "Tanks need infantry and engineers." Early in the Ukraine invasion, Russia's tanks tried

DISARMED

to advance into "urban environments without dismounted infantry support moving as screening and security for their vehicles." According to the Modern War Institute, "This lack of infantry presence allow[ed] Ukrainian forces to close with Russian armor and engage it directly with antitank weapons."[221]

The trick is, when the invaders leave their tanks, they're exposed. Breaking down how Ukraine managed to hold Kyiv, *The Washington Post* noted, "Without protection from armor, attacking troops are more vulnerable to small-arms fire from behind barricades and windows above."[222] Likewise, the *Military Times* reported that Ukrainians impeded the Russians with "simple moves such as putting disabled vehicles in major roadways or popping small arms fire whenever dismounted Russian troops [were] in the open."[223]

As the Ukrainians showed, you don't need an F-15 to repel an invading army. In urban warfare, small arms and homemade devices like Molotov cocktails can do the heavy lifting.

And Ukraine isn't an anomaly. The *Los Angeles Times* piece on urban warfare concluded, "History is full of examples of small, prepared urban defenders striking potent blows to a superior attacking military—including Mogadishu, Somalia, in 1993; Grozny, the Chechen capital, in 1994; and Suez City, Egypt, in 1973."[224] In Chechnya, for example, Russians troops struggled to overcome civilian resistance too. Chechens blocked the streets, just as Ukrainians did nearly thirty years later. They also dug trenches in Grozny's main street. The Russian tanks couldn't maneuver and had too little infantry support.[225]

The tables were turned in the famous Battle of Stalingrad in World War II. This time it was Russian and Soviet troops who held off a Nazi assault. A German bombing campaign had reduced the city to "a wilderness of ruin and rubble which is well-nigh impassable," a German lieutenant recounted in a letter home.[226] German tanks were "forced to sit on the sidelines," in the words of one historian. The "close proximity of the protagonists" limited "the use of air power and artillery," turning the Battle of Stalingrad into "an infantry action." A Soviet officer referred to it as the "Stalingrad Academy of Street Fighting."[227] Soviet snipers set up in the ruins and picked off German soldiers. One sniper killed 224 Germans; another, 185; still another, 149.[228]

Mad Max and MacGyver

It's not just in urban warfare where seemingly overmatched defenders can undercut the invaders' advantages in weaponry and manpower.

For example, Ukraine used equipment that looked like it came straight out of the movie *Mad Max*. Ukrainians made extensive use of "technicals," which are ordinary vehicles like pickup trucks customized with armor and guns. (Technicals became so common in the late stages of the war between Chad and Libya in the 1980s that the conflict became known as the Toyota War.) Technicals also emerged as a "backbone of the Ukrainian forces," in the words of the military news outlet *Task and Purpose*. They proved indispensable because "what technicals lack in armor and artillery power, they make up for in speed, maneuverability and ease of repair." They're also cheap and easy to find. *Task and Purpose* wrote that Ukraine's technicals featured "a truly wild array of weapons."[229] That array included, in addition to more advanced weapons like rocket-launch systems, things like automatic rifles and drones.

Think of it this way: when the more powerful Russians came, the Ukrainians MacGyvered the situation. Even with heavy weaponry coming in from other countries, Ukraine leveraged small arms to the hilt. That's exactly what anyone needs to do when they're outmanned and outgunned.

Why? One big reason is that small arms help you capture bigger guns, which in turn help you capture even more powerful weapons.

Ukraine discovered this benefit against Russia. When Russian troops retreated, they often left their weapons behind. In the village of Zaliznychne, for instance, hundreds of Russian soldiers fled from a Ukrainian counteroffensive "any way they could," including "on stolen bicycles" and "disguised as locals," *The Washington Post* reported. The soldiers simply dropped their rifles on the ground. They also left behind crates of ammunition and even a tank.[230]

Oryx is a Dutch website that provides open-source intelligence on military and defense. The site documents the military equipment that Russia has lost during the war with Ukraine, whether the equipment was abandoned, captured, or destroyed. Seven months into the war, Oryx tallied more than 1,800 vehicles, aircraft, and weapons that Ukraine had captured, and more than three hundred that the Russians had abandoned.[231] Those figures include:

- tanks (361 captured, 51 abandoned),
- armored fighting vehicles (159 captured, 29 abandoned),
- infantry fighting vehicles (384 captured, 73 abandoned),
- armored personnel carriers (73 captured, 9 abandoned),
- trucks, vehicles, and jeeps (365 captured, 53 abandoned),
- self-propelled anti-tank missile systems (11 captured, 5 abandoned),
- self-propelled artillery (78 captured, 13 abandoned),
- towed artillery (50 captured, 5 abandoned),
- multiple-rocket launchers (41 captured, 2 abandoned),
- anti-aircraft guns (8 captured),
- self-propelled anti-aircraft guns (5 captured, 3 abandoned), and
- surface-to-air missile systems (22 captured, 8 abandoned).

An NPR reporter said that Putin's soldiers abandoned so much weaponry that they spawned jokes about Ukraine's largest military supplier being Russia.[232] (Unfortunately, the United States became the Taliban's biggest arms supplier when President Biden fled Afghanistan, leaving behind at least $7 billion worth of weapons.)[233]

DISARMED

Soon the Ukraine-Russia dynamic stopped being a joke. In early October, a month into Ukraine's remarkably successful lightning offensive, *The Wall Street Journal* reported that Moscow had become "by far the largest supplier of heavy weapons for Ukraine, well ahead of the U.S. or other allies in sheer numbers."[234] Weapon captures both resulted from and contributed to Ukraine's offensive. The haul included Russian howitzers, tanks, and fighting vehicles. Taking these weapons from the Russians boosted the morale of Ukrainians, who referred to them as "trophies." But the captures also had a more direct impact on the war. One Ukrainian officer said: "The Russians no longer have a firepower advantage. We smashed up all their artillery units before launching the offensive, and then we started to move ahead so fast that they didn't even have time to fuel up and load their tanks. They just fled and left everything behind."[235]

Many other examples from history show that small arms help you to get more powerful weapons. One of the most famous cases occurred in the early days of the American Revolution. On May 10, 1775, fewer than a hundred Americans led by Benedict Arnold (who later became infamous as a traitor) and Ethan Allen of Vermont's Green Mountain Boys launched a surprise attack on Fort Ticonderoga, a British garrison in northeastern New York. Armed with little more than muskets, the Americans captured the fort—and all its cannons and other artillery. George Washington later ordered that artillery to be transferred to Boston. Once the Americans mounted the heavy guns on Dorchester Heights, outside of Boston, they forced the British to evacuate Boston.

So, yes, small arms matter. A lot.

"The Conventional Army Loses If It Does Not Win"

Ukraine's experience underscores a point that concerns the importance of small arms and civilian resistance: If you're protecting your homeland, you can keep traditional armies off-balance. You do it through irregular warfare.

That's what Ukrainians (professional soldiers, volunteers, and ordinary civilians alike) did when they fired rifles and hurled Molotov cocktails at Russian troops; when they blew up bridges and parked trucks and bulldozers in the middle of major roads to block the Russian advance; when they customized Toyotas, Fords, and Mitsubishis for battle; and when they blew up an important Russian ammunition depot.[236]

All this calls to mind a line from an article former Secretary of State Henry Kissinger wrote for *Foreign Affairs* in 1969. Assessing what had happened in the Vietnam War to that point, Kissinger wrote that the United States had "lost sight of one of the cardinal maxims of guerrilla war," which holds: "The guerrilla wins if he does not lose. The conventional army loses if it does not win."[237]

Think of how this maxim applies to Russia and Ukraine. Putin's original aim was (in the words of BBC News) "to sweep into the capital, Kyiv, in a matter of days and depose the government."[238] That's why Russia immediately went after Kyiv, the capital. Russia's initial strategy appeared similar to that of the United States in Vietnam, which Kissinger described as following "the classic doctrine that victory depended on a combination of control of territory and attrition of the opponent."[239]

Taking territory is hard enough on its own, as Russia's failed assault on Kyiv showed. But taking and *holding* territory when an armed populace is against you is incredibly hard. The British struggled during the American Revolution in part because the North American continent presented so much territory to cover. The British wanted to deliver a crushing blow to the Americans by seizing the capital, Philadelphia. They did so in September 1777, but the move did not have the desired effect. When Benjamin Franklin, stationed in Paris, heard the news that the British had taken Philadelphia, he responded, "No, sir, Philadelphia has taken the British."[240] Franklin's witty response turned out to be right. British troops couldn't get sufficient supplies to Philadelphia, since the Americans controlled the river leading into the city. Once the French joined the American side the next spring, the British knew they could not hold Philadelphia and evacuated.[241]

Ukraine is much smaller than the modern United States, but it still presents a lot of territory to cover. It is nearly the size of Texas and is the largest country located entirely in Europe.[242] The Center for Strategic and International Studies (CSIS) issued a detailed report that concluded, "The Russian invasion force was far too small to seize and hold territory, particularly with a Ukrainian population that rose up against the Russian military." Russia had between 150,000 and 190,000 soldiers for the invasion, meaning that it had a "force ratio" of about four Russian soldiers for every one thousand Ukrainians. The CSIS report continued:

> There are no exact formulas for how many soldiers are required to hold conquered territory, but a force ratio of as many as 20 soldiers per 1,000 inhabitants has sometimes been necessary to pacify a hostile local population.... In Iraq, for instance, the United States had 7 soldiers per 1,000 inhabitants and faced a persistent deadly insurgency—even with the help of Iraqi government forces and Sunni militia members.... In Afghanistan, the United States had only 1 soldier per 1,000 inhabitants, along with the help of Afghan National Security Forces. With such small numbers, the United States and its NATO allies faced a prolonged insurgency that led to the overthrow of the Afghan government in 2021.[243]

CSIS published that report in June 2022. Sure enough, in September, Russia lost control of more than four thousand square miles of territory it had previously captured, as Ukraine launched its lightning offensive.[244]

As for wearing down the opponent, that is, as Kissinger said, at least as much of a psychological and political matter as it is a military one.[245] And Ukraine's "spirit of national resistance" complicated Russia's attempts to erode the Ukrainians' will to fight.

The respected nonprofit research organization the RAND Corporation has reinforced the point that civilian resistance matters in more than strictly military cases. In 2021, RAND published a detailed analysis of "civilian-based resistance."[246] The authors looked at both armed and unarmed civilian resistance in the Baltic states from 1940 to 1991. The report found that civilians can help to prevent a population from succumbing to occupation through such measures as securing external support for the cause, maintaining and expanding popular support, and exposing the occupier's acts of violence and repression. But RAND also showed that civilians carrying small arms can impose "direct or indirect costs on an occupying force." After World War II, for example, armed civilians in Latvia carried out 2,700 attacks on Soviet occupiers. The Soviets needed to move at least sixty thousand soldiers to Lithuania to put down the resistance there.[247]

Planning and preparation of civilians for resistance during occupation should be done before an invasion takes place. In Ukraine, that was neglected too long. After the Ukrainians retook the city of Kherson, a partisan identifying himself as "Doron" described the lack of preparation before the Russian invasion:

> Before the full-scale invasion, he spoke to authorities about preparing for the Russians' arrival. He said that visiting the local territorial defense recruitment office left him very underwhelmed. "One guy was drunk. Another guy taped a knife to his leg with scotch tape," he recalled. According to Doron, Ukrainian intelligence left Kherson and other places poorly prepared to resist the Russians. Usually, when anticipating the possibility of captured territory and partisan resistance, hidden stashes of weapons and supplies should be prepared in advance. "There were no weapons, explosives, nothing in the areas that would be occupied," said Doron.[248]

But even when preparation is inadequate, armed civilian partisans can still impose substantial "direct or indirect costs on an occupying force." In Kherson, that was done by everything from sabotage to "sending targeting coordinates to assassinating ranking Russians and collaborators."[249]

Waiting Too Long

Now, you might think, *Well, a powerful conventional military can just carpet-bomb the resistance into submission.*

Not so fast. Overwhelming power doesn't always work.

Russia definitely ran into problems in Ukraine. The three warfare experts writing for the *Los Angeles Times* explained: "Russia discovered what many armies have learned from history: Bombing cities does not force their inhabitants to give up. It did not do so in the 1942 battle of Stalingrad, the 1945 battle of Berlin, or the 2003 U.S. invasion of Baghdad—ground forces must go in to clear and hold the city if it is to be taken."[250] Nor did it work in the Nazis' relentless bombing of British cities during the early part of World War II.

In fact, bombing cities can backfire. Remember that "wilderness of ruin and rubble" that Nazi Germany's bombing created in Stalingrad? The Nazis learned a painful lesson: as the *Los Angeles Times* essay put it, "Bombed buildings are easier to defend if a defender survives the initial bombing because rubble of concrete and steel makes for nifty bomb-proof bunkers to fight from and perfect locations to hide improvised explosive devices." This, then, is the paradox of urban warfare—"the more you bomb a city, the harder it is to take."[251]

Bombing leaves the conventional army vulnerable to even more forms of irregular warfare, including the kind that civilians carrying small arms can execute.

The limits of overwhelming force aren't confined to urban environments. As *The Atlantic* observed, "America bombed Vietnam for six years longer than it bombed Japan—and it still lost."[252] The United States and its allies dropped more than 7.5 million tons of bombs during that time.[253]

History is full of cases where overmatched forces held off or even defeated powerful militaries, keeping their land from being occupied. In the words of one historian, "From Algeria and Vietnam to Afghanistan, Chechnya, Lebanon, Somalia, and Iraq, insurgents have shown a consistent ability to humble great powers."[254] Actually, contrary to Joe Biden's claim that "you need F-15s and maybe some nuclear weapons" to take on regimes today, the historian points out that "guerrillas and terrorists have been growing more successful since 1945"—that is, precisely since the advent of the nuclear bomb.[255]

One historian characterized the Vietnam War as a contest between "B-52 bombers and bamboo traps," between "napalm and handguns," between "units of battalion strength and night patrols of five men."[256] We know how that turned out. As for Afghanistan, one of the greatest militaries in human history spent twenty years there and couldn't overcome Taliban forces equipped mostly with AK-47s and pickup trucks. There's a reason why Afghanistan is known as the Graveyard of Empires, and it's not because of sophisticated weaponry (well, not counting all the American weapons Biden left behind). Finally, when it comes to Iraq, all you need to do is ask, "What happened to 'shock and awe'?"[257]

Another fairly recent example comes from Sudan in Africa. During the 1990s, guerrilla fighters there took on the government's jihadist army. The guerrillas' mountain base was completely cut off from resupplies. "They had no vehicles, had no heavy weapons, and sometimes only had a handful of bullets each," in the words of an expert on Sudan.[258] But they still managed to hold their mountainous base.

DISARMED

Putin could have learned from his people's own history with Ukraine. In 1943, the Red Army launched an offensive in Ukraine. Ukrainians put up a fierce fight, much as they would eighty years later. A resistance movement known as the Ukrainian Insurgent Army (UPA) had come together to fight for independence. The Soviets ultimately put down the insurgency—but it took fourteen years! The Soviets suffered thousands of casualties at the hands of the UPA guerrillas, and the only way they could overcome the insurgency was by mobilizing tens of thousands of troops.[259]

And that wasn't the first time the Soviets struggled to put down a far less powerful opponent that relied on guerrilla tactics. In 1939, Joseph Stalin invaded neighboring Finland, intent on ousting the Finns' democratic government and installing a puppet regime. But "the war did not go as planned for the invaders," University of Virginia professor of politics Todd Sechser has recounted. "The outgunned Finnish army mounted a determined defense of their nation, surprising even themselves—and embarrassing the Red Army."[260]

Finland then (like Ukraine now) was an underdog for a reason. It eventually wore down and was forced to concede territory to Stalin. But the nation retained its independence, and it also sent a message to the Soviet Union. Sechser wrote: "Stalin learned that the Finns could—and would—put up a fight, even for seemingly small stakes. The Soviets lost more than 100,000 soldiers, several times more than the Finns. If the Soviets wanted to subdue Finland in the future, they knew it would be time-consuming and bloody."[261]

In other words, Finland established a strong deterrent effect, a matter we'll explore more in the next chapter.

Here's another example of the outsized impact a small force can have: During World War II, the Allies sent a team of nine men to sabotage Hitler's heavy-water facility in Norway. Neal Bascomb, author of an account of the raid, described the facility as "the only plant in the world that produced heavy water, which was the key ingredient in the German atomic bomb research program."[262] The mountainous fortress was heavily fortified with "minefields, searchlights, high barbed-wire fences, and constant patrols." But the Allies did not resort to bombing. In February 1942, the nine-man team braved sub-zero temperatures to cross the mountain plateau on skis before descending to a river valley and then climbing a five-hundred-foot-high cliff—"in the middle of the night, in the middle of winter!" The men infiltrated the plant and blew it up by planting explosives.[263]

Even today you hear the rallying cry "Remember the Alamo!" It doesn't mark a military victory. Rather, in 1836, a large Mexican army under the command of General Santa Anna took control of the Alamo Mission from a tiny band of Texas fighters. But the brave, undermanned resistance held off Santa Anna's assault for nearly two weeks. That resistance—as well as Santa Anna's cruelty—rallied support for the Texas cause. Just weeks later, Sam Houston and the Texans defeated Santa Anna's much bigger army at the Battle of San Jacinto. The Republic of Texas won its independence from Mexico.[264]

DISARMED

A few decades earlier, Napoleon had occupied parts of Spain and named his brother Joseph Bonaparte king of Spain. The Spanish launched insurrections in many areas, proving skilled at guerrilla tactics. An adviser to the king described the effect: "An invisible army spread itself over nearly the whole of Spain, like a net from whose meshes there was no escape for the French soldier who for a moment left his column or his garrison. Without uniforms and without weapons, apparently the guerrilleros escaped easily from the columns that pursued them, and it frequently happened that the troops sent out to do battle with them, passed through their midst without perceiving them."[265] The Spaniards' resistance drove King Joseph from the capital. Although the French counterattacked, the insurgents, along with British troops under the Duke of Wellington, wore down the French. The campaign in Spain marked the beginning of the end for the Napoleonic Empire.[266]

Or you can look at the American Revolution, when a ragtag army and civilian militias managed to defeat the mighty British Empire, which had the world's most powerful military at the time. From the very beginning, the Patriots employed irregular warfare and civilian communication networks. On the night of April 18, 1775, silversmith Paul Revere, tanner William Dawes, and doctor Samuel Prescott set out on horseback from Boston to alert fellow Patriots that the British were on the march to the town of Concord.[267]

Incidentally, you know the famous story of Revere's midnight ride in which he shouted, "The British are coming!" (Revere didn't actually use that line, but he did alert Patriots to the British advance.) But do you know why the British had set out for Concord? To seize an arms cache there.[268] They were trying to disarm the Patriots. That's why war broke out. Over gun control.

The Patriots who met the British regulars on Lexington Green were militia members—that is, able-bodied civilian men between the ages of sixteen and sixty. They brought their own guns. These civilians did not hold the Redcoats at Lexington, but the Minutemen forced the British to fall back at Concord. Even more important, they followed the British column all the way back to Boston, sniping from behind stone walls, houses, trees, and anything else they could find. The relentless attacks unnerved the British. Some Redcoats dropped their weapons to rush back to safety.[269]

It is also worth noting that both men and women contributed to the cause of American freedom during the Revolution. As historian Stephen Halbrook recounts, "Militia Colonel James Barrett's fifteen-year-old granddaughter Meliscent taught the other young women of the town how to assemble cartridges. And, after the skirmish at Lexington, the Redcoats marched on Concord, where they searched houses and destroyed arms and military stores. One account verified that 'even women had firelocks. One was seen to fire a blunderbuss between her father and husband from their windows.'"[270]

That initial day of fighting set the template for much of the Revolutionary War. Militiamen became known as "American hornets" for the way they would swarm and sting the British before disappearing just as quickly.[271] George Washington's crossing of the Delaware remains justly famous, but militia ambushes and raids inflicted most of the casualties that forced the British to flee New Jersey in 1777. A British general complained that "the whole country was now in arms." And in South Carolina, the "Swamp Fox," Francis Marion, wreaked havoc on the British with his raids.[272]

At least some Ukrainians drew inspiration from America's successful revolution. One militia volunteer, a young woman named Anna Sorochynska, delivered a message to Americans. "This year, 2022, is our 1783," she said, referring to the year Britain formally recognized U.S. independence.[273]

If you're looking for other examples, you could go all the way back to 480 B.C. That's when the valiant Spartans immortalized as "The 300" fought to the death to try to hold the Thermopylae pass against the vastly larger Persian army. Their heroics allowed most of the Greek troops to retreat successfully. Ultimately, the Greeks repelled the Persian invasion.[274]

The point is, it's not unusual for outmanned resisters to hold off powerful armies. Even in the direst situations, civilians have shown incredible valor and shocked mighty war machines with their resistance.

Take two examples of resistance against Nazi Germany. One occurred in the concentration camps of Sobibor and Treblinka. Prisoners there managed to steal guns from guards and launch revolts. The rebellions forced the Nazis to shut down these extermination camps. Those brave rebels probably didn't survive themselves, but they saved others' lives.²⁷⁵

The second example comes from the Warsaw ghetto uprising of 1943. A small group of Jewish fighters took on the Nazis to try to prevent being sent to the death camps. The resisters had little training and few weapons. Amazingly, it took nearly a month for the Nazis to put down the revolt. And the uprising inspired revolts in other ghettos.²⁷⁶

A Little Training Goes a Long Way

Anti-gun zealots insist that armed resistance to tyranny is futile. They couldn't be more wrong.

The best way to resist tyranny, or even to deter tyrants from attacking in the first place, is to ensure that your people are well trained in the use of guns. Justice Antonin Scalia put it well in the Supreme Court's landmark decision *District of Columbia v. Heller*: "When the able-bodied men of a nation are *trained* in arms and *organized*, they are better able to resist tyranny"²⁷⁷ (emphasis added).

The left-leaning publication *The Atlantic* put the matter bluntly: "If you want ordinary people to make your society occupation-proof, you have to teach them to kill well before they need to do so."²⁷⁸

This is a truth that Americans understood—in the past, at least.

America's Founders did more than enshrine the right to keep and bear arms in the Constitution. They made sure to give that right teeth, by passing laws *requiring* citizens to have arms and knowing how to use them.

Consider the Militia Act of 1792, which Congress passed only months after the states ratified the Second Amendment. This law required able-bodied free males between the ages of eighteen and forty-four to enroll in the militia. But Congress wasn't creating a standing army, with the federal government furnishing arms and supplies. No, the Militia Act obligated citizens to supply their own guns and ammunition. Specifically, it required every free and able-bodied male to "provide himself with a good musket or firelock, a sufficient bayonet and belt, two spare flints, and a knapsack, a pouch, with a box therein, to contain not less than twenty four cartridges." Or a militia member could show up with "a good rifle, knapsack, shot-pouch, and powder-horn, twenty balls suited to the bore of his rifle, and a quarter of a pound of powder."[279]

That's right: The law didn't just *allow* eighteen-year-olds to buy guns—something more and more states forbid today.[280] It *required* them to do so.

Nor was the federal Militia Act an aberration. As far back as the seventeenth century, Massachusetts required militia members to carry a "good fixed musket" and "twenty bullets."[281] New Hampshire passed a similar law in 1716.[282] In 1742, Delaware obligated "every Freeholder and taxable Person" to "provide himself" with "one well fixed Musket or Firelock, one Cartouch-Box, with Twelve Charges of Gun-Powder and Ball therein."[283]

After America won its independence, states passed laws in the same vein. To take only one example, Virginia required noncommissioned officers and privates to have a "good clean musket," "one pound of powder," and "four pounds of lead." The Virginia law's name clearly stated its purpose: for "Regulating and Disciplining the Militia, and *Guarding Against Invasions and Insurrections*"[284] (emphasis added).

Although the early structure of militias faded away, the belief in the importance of training did not. In fact, the National Rifle Association (NRA) was founded specifically to fill the gap and ensure that Americans knew how to handle weapons. Only six years after the Civil War ended, two Union veterans, Colonel William Church and General George Wingate, started the NRA because they were "dismayed by the lack of marksmanship shown by their troops."[285] The NRA soon built a rifle range as a practice ground and to host shooting competitions. By the early twentieth century, the NRA was hosting training and competitions for young men and women. The organization established shooting clubs at colleges and universities across the country.

Around the same time, political leaders acted to ensure proper firearms training. In 1903, Congress and President Theodore Roosevelt established the National Board for the Promotion of Rifle Practice, the forerunner to today's Civilian Marksmanship Program. The government acted "to strengthen our country's national defense capabilities by improving the rifle marksmanship skills of members of the Armed Forces," in the words of the Civilian Marksmanship Program history.[286] Over time, the program shifted its focus from military marksmanship to "training civilians who might serve in the military." Today, it focuses on "developing youth through marksmanship training." Whereas the Department of the Army ran the program for nearly a century, today's Civilian Marksmanship Program operates as a nonprofit organization chartered by Congress. The organization began hosting shooting competitions at Ohio's Camp Perry in 1907, and continues to do so today.[287]

As admirable as these programs are, they reach a much smaller percentage of the population than did training efforts in the eighteenth and nineteenth centuries.

That fact alone should give us some concern. Here again, Ukraine stands as a cautionary tale, no matter how much the country exceeded expectations against Russia. Ukraine's eleventh-hour legislation letting citizens carry firearms was a symptom of a broader problem: the government's failure not only to allow civilians to handle weapons but also to ensure they had adequate firearms training. In *The Atlantic*'s words, Ukrainian leaders "failed badly" by "waiting too long to arm and train their citizens."[288]

Some Ukrainians took it upon themselves to train after Russia's annexation of Crimea. A *New Yorker* reporter described meeting a Territorial Defense Forces unit soon after Russia invaded Ukraine. "The volunteers did not look particularly impressive—they were older, and some of them were out of shape," the reporter wrote. But the men had formed a "civilian sniper club" in 2015 and "had gathered on weekends to practice marksmanship, outdoor skills, combat medicine, and even 'tactical alpinism.' (A sudden urban assault might require them to rappel from their apartment buildings.)"[289]

What if Ukraine had formally organized the Territorial Defense Forces years earlier and supplied firearms training? That's what Finland does, as the respected military strategist Edward Luttwak points out. In Finland, "adolescent males report for a short and intense period of military training, followed by shorter refreshers for most of their adult life." This focused training doesn't aim to produce military professionals. Instead, "it prepares civilians to be ready to join their unit and harass and kill invaders." Luttwak also notes how civilians with small arms can fight a tyrannical force: "Once the tank stops rolling forward, let the soldiers come out to cook or to pee, and then kill them."[290]

Russia's invasion of Ukraine put Finland on even higher alert. Like Ukraine, Finland shares a border with Russia. And like Ukraine, Finland has endured Russian aggression before. During the Cold War and after, Finland took pains not to antagonize Russia. That changed once Russia invaded Ukraine. Finland began considering NATO membership, angering Putin. And the day of the invasion, Finland's president said: "Now masks have been removed. Only the cold face of war is visible."[291] For nearly thirty years, the Finnish Reservists' Association has offered wartime defense courses for civilians. The courses have always been popular, but after the invasion of Ukraine, enrollment spiked. One official who had been with the Reservists' Association from the beginning said: "The change has been enormous. It's something very special. I haven't seen anything like this before." A reservist who led some training sessions said of the huge demand for the courses: "I wouldn't call it fear. It's more about being prepared."[292]

Finland isn't alone either. Russia's attack on Ukraine spurred new preparations in Taiwan as well. Three months after the invasion, the *Los Angeles Times* reported:

> For decades, Taiwan has lived under the specter of military aggression from mainland China, which considers the self-ruled island as part of its territory. But it wasn't until Russia invaded Ukraine in February that many Taiwanese started wondering what role they might play if a war broke out at home and Chinese soldiers were suddenly on the beaches.[293]

Unlike Finland, though, Taiwan didn't have a strong tradition of firearms training or preparedness. As the *Los Angeles Times* put it, the instinct to learn how to use weapons "has run up against strict gun-control laws and a complicated history between [Taiwan's] people and military, dating back to the days of martial law under the Nationalist Party, or Kuomintang." An instructor in one of Taiwan's beginner shooting classes explained the view of Taiwanese society: "Guns were an evil thing. You didn't want to come into contact with them."²⁹⁴ But enrollment in his classes tripled after Russia invaded Ukraine. With a threatening China looming, many Taiwanese didn't want to be caught as unprepared as Ukrainians had been.

In examining the Finnish model, *The Atlantic* concluded, "A territorial-defense reserve can deter occupation in the first place—particularly if it has training and enjoys the logistical support of other countries."²⁹⁵

Indeed, as we'll see in the next chapter, the mere fact that people have arms and know how to use them can be a powerful deterrent. Why do you think so many totalitarian regimes have been eager to disarm the people?

5

THE DETERRENCE FACTOR (OR: WHY TYRANTS DISARM THE PEOPLE)

Let's return to a question raised in Chapter 3: How might the situation in Ukraine have turned out differently had Ukrainian leaders preemptively protected the people's right to keep and bear arms, kept the country's weapons supply, and taken firearms training more seriously?

Again, the obvious answer is that Ukraine would have been much better prepared to counter the Russian invasion. Ukrainians, with their spirit of national resistance, managed to protect Kyiv and score other surprising successes *despite* their lack of preparation. Imagine how much better the war efforts could have gone had Ukraine not scrambled together the Territorial Defense Forces only weeks before the invasion; had civilians not needed to descend *en masse* to gun stores at the last minute; had they received real firearms training, not emergency lessons using wooden cutouts.

But let's also consider the possibility that if Ukraine had had a well-armed population prepared to use guns, and if the country had had substantial Territorial Defense Forces trained and ready, Russia might not have invaded in the first place.

We're talking about deterrence. It's a lesson Finland learned, as described in the previous chapter.

Now, is there any guarantee that a sufficiently armed and prepared Ukraine would have kept Russia from attacking? No, of course not. Nothing is certain when dealing with a leader like Vladimir Putin. It's clear that Putin badly underestimated the Ukrainians' capacity to respond and overestimated Russia's capabilities.[296] Perhaps nothing would have kept him from pursuing his obsession with bringing Ukraine back under Russia's heel.

But deterrence is a real and vital factor when it comes to dealing with a threat, whether from abroad or at home. Leaders have understood the importance of deterrence for millennia. The idea of "peace through strength" dates as far back as the Roman emperor Hadrian in the second century.[297]

That phrase, which Ronald Reagan invoked, is often associated with major arms buildups—the stockpiling of missiles, nuclear weapons, and fighter jets. But such arms are not the only way to build strength.

DISARMED

Months before war erupted in Ukraine, a military historian wrote, "The threat of guerrilla warfare is the most potent deterrent to a Russian invasion of Ukraine, and it is one that Ukraine and its supporters in the West need to play up to make Putin think twice before he launches another war of aggression."[298] But Ukraine and its allies waited to react until after the invasion was imminent.

President George Washington emphasized preparedness as well as the importance of an armed citizenry. In his first State of the Union address, Washington said, "To be prepared for war is one of the most effectual means of preserving peace."[299] Here, Washington echoed the fourth-century Roman military expert Vegetius, who wrote, "*Qui desiderat pacem, praeparet bellum*"—"Let him who desires peace, prepare for war," or as it's often translated, "If you want peace, prepare for war."[300] The aphorism comes from Vegetius's work *Rei militaris instituta*, which has been called "the single most influential military treatise in the Western world."[301] Washington owned and annotated a copy of the famous treatise.[302]

Four years after that State of the Union address, President Washington said, "If we desire to avoid insult, we must be able to repel it; if we desire to secure peace, one of the most powerful instruments of our rising prosperity, it must be known that we are at all times ready for war."[303] Washington called on Congress to add to the "amount and kinds of arms and military stores now in our magazines and arsenals." He also spoke of the importance of militias, "who ought to possess a pride in being the depository of the force of the

Republic."[304] Washington concluded, "A free people ought not only to be armed but disciplined."[305]

That's still true in the twenty-first century. Once again, Ukraine provides an object lesson for anyone interested in understanding how to resist tyranny. An analysis in the *Military Times* concluded, "While Ukraine was unable to deter Russia's invasion, the impact of these volunteers in the current war may serve as a deterrent to future wars."[306]

The authors of that analysis, both experts on modern warfare, traveled to Ukraine to interview "dozens of Ukrainian Army, Territorial Defense Force, and civilian volunteers" and to visit "dozens of sites." They observed that Ukraine's volunteer forces included men and women from across Ukrainian society, ranging from teenagers to sexagenarians. The "vast majority" would "never pass the physical fitness tests of the U.S. Army," and yet "they pulled off a feat almost unparalleled in modern warfare: they helped defeat one of the largest standing armies in the world and held the capital."[307]

But again, they managed these achievements despite their government's lack of preparation. Whenever the *Military Times* saw volunteers with good weapons, the volunteers said they had retrieved the arms from Russian forces. "Often, it was the only way for volunteers to get machine guns and RPGs [rocket-propelled grenades] since the Ukrainian Army lacked sufficient numbers of these weapons to distribute to volunteers."[308]

An ounce of prevention is worth a pound of cure, Benjamin Franklin famously said. Ukraine didn't remember this wisdom soon enough, but other countries are learning. And they know that deterrence and preparedness depend on civilians.

Volunteers Strengthen Deterrence

Ukrainians didn't prepare enough for the 2022 invasion even though they had seen Vladimir Putin act on his aggressive intentions in 2014. Other countries did heed the lessons of that experience, though.

For example, the Baltic states of Estonia, Latvia, and Lithuania began preparing deterrent measures. Their planning took on greater urgency in 2016, when the RAND Corporation reported on war-gaming exercises it had run. In the words of the Modern War Institute at West Point, the RAND report "found that Russian forces could seize any of the three Baltic capitals within 36–60 hours—faster than NATO could deploy troops to support."[309]

So how did these countries seek to deter Russia? They didn't get into an arms race. They knew they could never compete, not when Russia's defense budget exceeded each country's entire gross domestic product.[310]

No, the Baltic states incorporated volunteers—civilians—into their defense planning. As the Modern War Institute explained, they focused on "arming civilian militias and volunteer reserve forces" and teaching "civilians how to fight like guerrillas." These nations viewed volunteers "as a cost-effective deterrent that contributes to a 'porcupine' or 'poison pill' strategy." The goal of the strategy was "to convince a would-be invader that it would be too costly in the long term for the invader to maintain their gains," with the hope that this understanding would deter the enemy "from invading in the first place."[311]

Here countries are taking a conscious approach to what the previous chapter called irregular warfare, or what the great Prussian military strategist Carl von Clausewitz called indirect warfare. The goal, as the Modern War Institute put it, "is to exhaust the enemy." The military analysts from the institute explained that "this strategy proved effective for the Viet Cong against the U.S. in Vietnam and for the mujahideen in Afghanistan against the Soviet Union in the 1980s."[312] Exhausting the invader is another way of expressing Kissinger's "cardinal maxim" of guerilla warfare: "The guerrilla wins if he does not lose. The conventional army loses if it does not win."[313]

And it proved effective again for Ukraine when Russia invaded, three years after the Modern War Institute analysis appeared.

Thus, as the *Military Times* writers concluded, "The Battle of Kyiv proved that volunteers could shape the course of a war, which holds important implications for the future of war."[314]

DISARMED

Armed Neutrality—Emphasis on *Armed*

The Baltic states aren't alone in developing a well-armed and well-trained citizenry as a deterrent. As we've seen, Finland emphasizes the role of reservists in territorial defense. The Finnish Defense Forces have only about twenty-three thousand active personnel, but they can call on *nine hundred thousand* reservists. By contrast, neighboring Sweden has almost the same number of active personnel but only 31,800 reservists.[315]

The point of Finland's territorial-defense reserve is, as *The Atlantic* said, to "deter occupation in the first place."[316] It's easy to understand why the Finns prioritize deterrence. Finland had been part of the Russian Empire before it declared independence in 1917. Since then, Russian or Soviet forces have invaded Finland three times. The two countries share a border that extends more than eight hundred miles.[317]

The question is not so much why Finland has gone to these lengths, as it is why other countries, such as Ukraine, have not.

Another nation that emphasizes deterrence through an armed citizenry is Switzerland. The Swiss are famous for their long-held position of "armed neutrality." The "armed" part is crucial; they couldn't maintain their neutrality without it. "Switzerland has a militia army with a limited number of professional soldiers," the Swiss Broadcasting Corporation reports. "Under the constitution, military service is compulsory for male citizens, whereas it is optional for women."³¹⁸ That service lasts about twenty-one weeks initially, but the Swiss go back for short refresher courses.

The system means, first and foremost, that a large part of Switzerland's population knows how to handle guns—and *has* guns, too. As BBC News explains, "All healthy Swiss men aged between 18 and 34 are obliged to do military service and all are issued with assault rifles or pistols which they are supposed to keep at home."³¹⁹ Until relatively recently they were *required* to keep their guns and ammunition at home.³²⁰ Admiral James Stavridis, the former NATO supreme allied commander, praises Switzerland's "exceptional" and "incredibly ready reserves." Stavridis adds, "The military tradition there is deeply respected and woven into Swiss culture."³²¹

It's no accident that Switzerland hasn't been invaded in centuries despite many European wars.³²² Belgium was neutral too, but it was invaded in both world wars. A European think tank recently explained that Germany was able to violate Belgium's neutrality easily because Belgium lacked Switzerland's "armed deterrence capabilities" and its "culture of military resistance."³²³

Historian Stephen Halbrook wrote a book on the importance of Swiss armed neutrality in World War II. Why did Switzerland avoid Nazi occupation? Halbrook noted that the Swiss had a "fierce determination to resist any threats to their independence, particularly in the form of ideologies wholly foreign to the Swiss experience." In Switzerland, "sovereignty began with the individual, not the central authorities." Oh, and "every man kept a rifle for the defense of his home, his family, his canton, and, finally, Switzerland itself."[324] Halbrook concluded that Switzerland "deterred invasion by the most powerful and aggressive totalitarian state in modern European history" through its "centuries-old policy of active, armed neutrality" combined with its "war-time mobilization and armament."[325]

Not a bad record.

Of course, for either deterrence or armed resistance to work, citizens and the military must actually have guns, as the Swiss do. It's another area in which Ukraine was woefully underprepared. Part of the problem, as we've seen, is that the country disposed of so much of its weapons inventory thanks to then-senator Barack Obama. Also, the restrictive gun control laws in Ukraine severely limited the civilian market for guns, and civilians were not incorporated into Ukraine's defense forces. Thus, the domestic firearms manufacturing base in Ukraine was extremely limited. To obtain small arms in sufficient numbers, Ukraine had to look abroad.

It's not that Ukraine is unable to manufacture its own firearms. A company located there, called Zbroyar, makes a good quality variant of the AR-15 rifle designated as the Z-15 (which shoots .223/5.56 mm rounds). It also makes a variant of the AR-10 called the Z-10 (which shoots more powerful 7.62 x 51mm rounds) and is used as a sniper rifle.[326] It's likely that Ukraine's domestic production of small arms has increased during the war, but it would have been very helpful, to say the least, to have had a healthy domestic manufacturing base and widespread, legal civilian ownership of firearms prior to the war.

We should remember that in the United States as well. Back in the late 1990s and early 2000s, anti-gun jurisdictions with bottomless pockets began suing major firearms manufacturers with the hope of driving them out of business either through damages awards or the sheer cost of relentless litigation. Frivolous lawsuits became such a problem that Congress in 2005 passed the Protection of Lawful Commerce in Arms Act (PLCAA), which banned such abusive suits. Congress recognized that destruction of our domestic small arms industry would cripple our military abilities. To what foreign power can America turn for help if we find ourselves in a major war after our own firearms makers have been litigated out of existence? There won't be one.

That's why the U.S. Department of Defense endorsed the PLCAA when Congress was considering the bill. The Defense Department issued a statement saying it "strongly supports" the bill's passage because the law would "help safeguard our national security by limiting unnecessary lawsuits against an industry that plays a critical role in meeting the procurement needs of our men and women in uniform."[327] But recently the anti-gun crowd thinks it has found a way around the PLCAA, and the litigation has resumed. Among the lessons we should draw from the Ukraine war is the vital importance of preserving our national firearms manufacturing industry.

DISARMED

Disarmament: The Tyrant's Not-So-Secret Weapon

If you really want to see how powerful a deterrent armed citizens can be, consider this fact: tyrants throughout history have routinely disarmed the people.

As law professor Nelson Lund put it, "Governments bent on the oppression of their people almost always disarm the civilian population before undertaking more drastically oppressive measures."[328] Similarly, David B. Kopel, an expert on constitutional law and firearms, and two other scholars have written: "The historical record shows that, almost without exception, genocide is preceded by a very careful government program that disarms the future victims. Genocide is almost never attempted against an armed population."[329]

These scholars echo a point that the great Supreme Court justice Joseph Story made in the nineteenth century. Story wrote, "One of the ordinary modes, by which tyrants accomplish their purposes without resistance, is, by disarming the people, and making it an offence to keep arms."[330]

Adolf Hitler agreed, though of course he looked on disarming enemies approvingly. Hitler told his inner circle:

> *The most foolish mistake we could possibly make would be to allow the subject races to possess arms. History shows that all conquerors who have allowed their subject races to carry arms have prepared their own downfall by so doing. Indeed, I would go so far as to say that the*

supply of arms to the underdogs is a sine qua non for the overthrow of any sovereignty.[331]

Not surprisingly, Hitler's Germany disarmed political enemies at home as well as the peoples it conquered. The Third Reich disarmed Jews, paving the way for Kristallnacht. When the Nazis occupied France, they ordered that anyone who didn't turn in their guns within twenty-four hours would be executed. During the Nazi occupation of Czechoslovakia, the Gestapo raided homes to determine whether families were harboring not only Jews but guns as well.[332]

Disarming the people has been part of tyrants' and conquerors' playbooks for millennia. "When the Philistines conquered the Hebrews, they disarmed them," Kopel writes. "The tyrant Peisistratus of ancient Athens seized political power by disarming the people. When King James II of England was trying to assume despotic powers, he worked to disarm the English people, other than his reliable political supporters."[333]

The British later tried to disarm American colonies. As noted, the Revolutionary War began when British troops marched to Concord to raid a Patriot arms cache. Barely a day after "the shot heard 'round the world," the royal governor of Virginia ordered British troops to seize the gunpowder in Williamsburg. The soldiers also destroyed guns there.[334] And British general Thomas Gage said that Bostonians could leave town freely if they "temporarily" deposited their guns, allegedly for safekeeping. Bostonians turned in nearly 2,700 guns. Then the British seized all the weapons and refused to let anyone

DISARMED

leave.[335] In 1777, British Undersecretary of State William Knox circulated a proposal for what to do with America: "The Militia Laws should be repealed and none suffered to be re-enacted, & the Arms of all the People should be taken away, & every piece of Ordnance removed into the King's Stores."[336]

The British began disarming Americans well before Lexington and Concord. In 1768, the *Boston Gazette* published an account (probably written by Samuel Adams) that said the British had commanded "that the Inhabitants of this Province are to be disarmed." The *Gazette* called this action "more grievous to the People than any Thing hitherto made known."[337] Then, in 1774, the British banned imports of firearms and gunpowder. British troops also began disarming colonists and local governments. In a September incident known as the Powder Alarm, Redcoats seized hundreds of barrels of gunpowder in Boston. Some twenty thousand militiamen started marching toward Boston when rumors spread that shooting had broken out. The British then ordered warrantless searches and seizures of guns and ammunition, which continued into 1775. The *Boston Gazette* observed that of all the British offenses, the seizure of arms and ammunition was "what most irritated the People."[338]

That disarmament strategy is not limited to Western cultures. Toyotomi Hideyoshi was one of the most powerful military and political figures in Japan in the sixteenth century. In 1588, he proclaimed the *katanagari*, or "sword hunt," in which swords were confiscated. His edict prohibited everyone but the samurai class from possessing "any swords, short swords, bows, spears, firearms or other types of weapons," and exhorted non-samurai to convert those "precious swords and sharp knives into agricultural implements...."[339] The stated reason was his "compassionate concern for the well-being of the farmers," and disarming them would supposedly ensure the "peace and security of the country and the joy and happiness of all the people."[340] Sound familiar? In fact, "to consolidate the power of the ruling class, peasants' swords had to be taken away."[341]

The trend of tyrants and conquerors disarming the people accelerated in the twentieth century, the bloodiest in recorded history. Soon after the Bolsheviks seized power in Russia, they issued a declaration calling for "the complete disarmament of the wealthy classes."[342] The same declaration called for arming the working classes, but only months later, the Council of People's Commissars decreed that "the entire population" must surrender its arms. Anyone who didn't turn in his weapons would be "subject to imprisonment."[343] The Soviets used their secret police to seize those arms.

Thus disarmed, the people could do little to resist the communist regime. Over about a quarter century, the Soviets rounded up more than twenty million people and sent them to the Gulag, their vast system of labor camps, or into exile.[344] The most famous Gulag prisoner, Nobel Prize winner Aleksandr Solzhenitsyn, reflected on his and others' inability to resist. In *The Gulag Archipelago*, Solzhenitsyn wrote:

> And how we burned in the camps later, thinking: What would things have been like if every Security operative,

when he went out at night to make an arrest, had been uncertain whether he would return alive and had to say good-bye to his family? Or if, during periods of mass arrests, as for example in Leningrad, when they arrested a quarter of the entire city, people had not simply sat there in their lairs, paling with terror at every bang of the downstairs door and at every step on the staircase, but had understood they had nothing left to lose and had boldly set up in the downstairs hall an ambush of half a dozen people with axes, hammers, pokers, or whatever else was at hand?... The Organs would very quickly have suffered a shortage of officers and transport and, notwithstanding all of Stalin's thirst, the cursed machine would have ground to a halt!

If...if... We didn't love freedom enough.[345]

The Soviets also forcibly disarmed the people in Chechnya and Dagestan.[346] Ukraine suffered from Soviet disarmament too. The esteemed historian Robert Conquest relates how, under Joseph Stalin, the Soviets made a "great effort" to "prevent the [Ukrainian] peasantry from possessing arms." They required Ukrainians to register their firearms—which made it easy for the Soviets to round up all the weapons later.[347]

Kopel has noted the "vigor with which the Warsaw Pact dictatorships enforced gun control." He explains:

> When the Communists took over Bulgaria on September 9, 1944, they immediately confiscated every weapon in private possession. In East Germany, private gun ownership was outlawed, although citizens were allowed to rent hunting guns for one-day periods. Immediately after World War II, Hungary was governed by a coalition of democrats and Communists. Preparing the way for a total Communist takeover, Laszlo Rajk, the Communist Minister of the Interior, ordered the dissolution of all pistol and hunting clubs, as well as of other organizations which might prove a threat to government power. Rajk claimed he acted "in order to more efficiently protect the democratic system of the state."[348]

Mao's Chinese Communists confiscated guns almost immediately after seizing power.[349] So did Fidel Castro's regime in Cuba and the Khmer Rouge in Cambodia.[350]

In all, governments murdered more than two hundred million people in the twentieth century. That staggering figure does *not* include battle deaths from wars. The "overwhelming majority" of those murdered, Kopel concludes, were "victims who had been assiduously disarmed by dictatorships before the killing began."[351]

The disarmament trend has continued in the twenty-first century. Sudan's Islamist regime paved the way for its genocide in Darfur by disarming non-Arab ethnic groups.[352] Under authoritarian strongmen Hugo Chavez and Nicolás Maduro, Venezuela banned the sale of firearms and ammunition to civilians. The law explicitly declared its goal: to "disarm all citizens."[353] After Venezuela imposed this supposed public-safety measure, violent crimes and murders soared.[354] In 2021, *The New York Times* reported, "With Venezuela in shambles, criminals and insurgents run large stretches of the nation's territory."[355] The country descended into such a state of lawlessness that it landed near the very bottom of Gallup's 2022 Law and Order Index, ahead of only Gabon (barely) and Afghanistan.[356] The gun ban also left Venezuelans defenseless against the dictatorial regime. In a single year, government forces shot and killed almost two hundred pro-democracy protesters.[357]

But somehow anti-gun activists insist that the United States needs to ban entire classes of firearms and ammunition magazines, restrict the constitutional right to carry arms, and create gun registries—all in the name of "public safety."

If we're not willing to learn from Ukraine's experience, perhaps the long line of other examples should alert us to the dangers of sacrificing our right to armed self-defense. As Joseph Story said, the Second Amendment serves as a "powerful check upon the designs of ambitious men."[358]

Lack of Arms Dooms Resistance to Tyranny

You can clearly see the dangers of giving up the right to keep and bear arms when you consider the attempted revolts against tyranny that failed because the people had been disarmed.

As liberal law professor Sanford Levinson has acknowledged, "A state facing a totally disarmed population is in a far better position, for good or ill, to suppress popular demonstrations and uprisings than one that must calculate the possibilities of its soldiers and officials being injured or killed."[359]

Think, in particular, of the failed uprisings behind the Iron Curtain: East Germany in 1953, Hungary in 1956, and Czechoslovakia in 1968. The Soviet Union's Red Army crushed these revolts. "One reason that the Soviet army succeeded in those bloody episodes of subjugation," Kopel writes, "was that the people of East Germany, Hungary, and Czechoslovakia lacked the arms with which to fight a guerilla war."[360]

The Czechs, for example, could offer almost no armed resistance when several hundred thousand Soviet-led troops invaded Czechoslovakia to crush the liberal reforms known as the "Prague Spring."[361] They had to rely on nonviolent protest and simple acts of sabotage like removing road signs to confuse the Red Army.[362]

Compare that to the experience in the Hungarian Revolution a dozen years earlier. That uprising, too, ended in brutal suppression by the Red Army. But "at certain points," one historical account notes, "the revolt looked like it was on the verge of an amazing triumph."[363]

DISARMED

How did the Hungarians put up such a fierce fight? First, they displayed strong will, fighting "often armed with nothing more than kitchen implements and gasoline."[364] But they also got their hands on some guns. Factories around Budapest made munitions for communist armies. As workers in those factories rose up, they took guns and ammunition to their fellow rebels. Hungarians serving in the communist regime's security force didn't stop the uprising; some even handed weapons over to the rebels. And those guns helped them to get more and bigger guns. Some Soviet soldiers dropped their weapons and fled (just as Russian soldiers did in Ukraine).[365] In a first-person account written in the present tense, a Hungarian news photographer recounted, "The weapons, whether from Hungarian army stores or captured in the fighting, are Russian—the Russians are being shot by their own bullets."[366]

As it turned out, the seized weapons weren't enough. But the fact that the Hungarians had any success at all is remarkable. And that success came about because they gained access to *some* firearms. This is yet another reminder of the importance of an armed citizenry. Had the Hungarians and the Czechs been better armed, Kopel writes, "Eastern Europe might not have had to wait until 1989 for the Kremlin's permission to be free."[367]

There is no question that they wanted to be free. A bitter Cold War joke behind the Iron Curtain went like this: "Q: Why do the Czechs pour motor oil into their flower gardens? A: To keep the guns from rusting." But, having been disarmed for three straight decades, first by the Nazis and then by the communists, there weren't enough of those guns for the Czechs to stand a chance against the Red Army in 1968.

A year after the Warsaw Ghetto uprising, a broader based Polish resistance movement rose up against the Nazis. The Polish Home Army, known as the AK, led this resistance. The AK and its supporters launched Operation Tempest, a series of uprisings across Poland throughout 1944. Don't let the word "army" in the group's name fool you. The members of this resistance movement didn't have many weapons either. By the time they made their move in Warsaw that summer, they had, a Polish historian reports, "minimal arms"—only several thousand rifles and pistols.[368] Most of their weapons they had made themselves, in underground workshops.[369] Meanwhile, their ammunition supply "looked catastrophic."[370] The Warsaw district commander said that any rebels without arms would receive "axes, hoes, [and] crowbars."[371]

The historian comments, "It is hard to comprehend today how the Warsaw district commander wanted to conduct an extensive attack against the Germans with the weapons available to his units."[372] But two points here:

First, the commander acknowledged that the Polish resistance was "too weak to destroy the opponent." He wasn't calling for a frontal assault; he was talking about street fighting and the kind of irregular warfare that can disrupt even the mightiest army.

The second point is broader—and for our purposes, probably more important: What other choice did the Polish have? This is exactly the kind of desperation, the kind of lesser-of-two-evils thinking, that you're left with when you don't have the arms and ammunition you need to defend yourself.

The NRA earned criticism and mockery when, in 1989, it tied a lack of gun rights to Communist China's massacre of thousands of student demonstrators in and around Tiananmen Square. Because the Chinese regime denied people the right to keep and bear arms, the NRA said, the brave pro-democracy protesters "could only hurl words and hold out empty hands against an army."[373]

Some scholars have noted that the NRA had a point. Fordham University law professor Nicholas Johnson, for instance, has written about Tiananmen Square while discussing the dangers of a disarmed citizenry. Johnson argues that denying the people gun rights looms as a "structural constitutional threat" because "significant abuse of collective power is more likely to occur against a disarmed citizenry." When the people are disarmed, they are left with "abstract rhetorical limitations on collective power," which present "weak barriers to abuse." In this context, Johnson cites the "valiant but crushed efforts of pro-democracy protesters in Tiananmen Square." He adds:

> *One can conjure up images of massive passive resistance and noble sacrifices in the vein of Tiananmen Square; however, these images ignore the power of bluff. The threat of force and its moderate implementation against*

unarmed groups is a highly effective and relatively low-cost tactic. Contrast this with the type of government violence against citizens that would be necessary to truly overwhelm an armed populace. True, government will have a monopoly on weapons of mass destruction, but the decision to use those on a domestic civilian population is much less likely than the decision simply to show and threaten force.[374]

David Kopel writes: "Peaceful, unarmed mass protesters can be murdered *en masse* if the government has the nerve and a compliant military. The Chinese Communist Party so demonstrated in Beijing's Tiananmen Square."[375] He explains, "Against the armed force of the People's Liberation Army, [the Tiananmen Square protesters] knew their only hope was the moral force of nonviolence."[376] Kopel adds another example: "Venezuela's communist regime has been demonstrating the same point for years, using its armed forces—including the government-armed *collectivo* gangsters—to suppress and kill demonstrators."[377]

Maybe the most important takeaway from Ukraine today, Poland in World War II, or any of these other cases is that they show the absurdity of the anti-gun mantra of "Who really needs [this kind of weapon, or that much ammunition]?" Ask anyone who has confronted a real threat. They'll tell you that you can never have enough guns and ammunition.

DISARMED

Localized Forms of Tyranny and Terror

Okay, but you may be thinking, *Come on, we don't have the Red Army or the Wehrmacht marching on our cities. And we're not living under a murderous regime.*

Well, of course. But remember the warnings Ukrainians have given us. In the opening chapter, we heard reporter and author George Packer (who has endorsed gun control in the United States) say of his experience in Ukraine that "the essential things—to be free and live with dignity—became clear." Packer added, "It almost seemed as if the U.S. would have to be attacked or undergo some other catastrophe for Americans to remember what Ukrainians have known from the start." And a prominent Ukrainian novelist said: "It's a bad idea to have to face invasion in order to remember values. Not recommended by those who experience it."[378]

That's precisely right. The goal of this book is to amplify such warnings, so we don't ever find ourselves unprepared and regretting our mistakes, like Ukraine.

And yes, we should prepare for various scenarios, no matter how unlikely they may seem now. Black Swan events happen.

It's equally important to realize that tyrannical regimes or foreign invaders don't represent the only conceivable threats. Americans face plenty of real dangers every single day, including crime, gangs, armed illegal aliens, and states where gun-control laws make it difficult for the law-abiding to own firearms. You might think of these as localized forms of tyranny.

As I said in the first chapter, having guns and ammunition, knowing how to use them, and retaining the legal right to use them offer the best defense against tyranny and terror of any kind.

You never know when evil will appear. It comes at inconvenient times. The aggressor picks his time to attack; you won't be consulted. Do you want to end up like the people of Venezuela, disarmed and defenseless? Or do you want to be able to protect yourself, your family, your community, or even, if need be, your country?

I know my answer—especially when I look around and see what's happening. In 2020, the United States recorded the highest single-year increase in the homicide rate in *more than a century*.[379] That year also brought 4.5 million violent crimes.[380]

Despite the spike in murders and the prevalence of violent crime, the "defund the police" movement left law enforcement in a state of unprecedented weakness. In 2020, New York City saw a 58 percent increase in homicides—while the city logged 38 percent fewer arrests.[381] In Chicago, murders jumped 65 percent while arrests dropped 53 percent.[382] After Portland, Oregon, defunded the police to the tune of $12 million, shootings jumped 173 percent and murders surged 255 percent.[383] In 2021, at least a dozen major American cities set all-time records for homicides.[384] There has also been a strong push by leftist politicians and activists to reduce prison sentences, even though more than 70 percent of released prisoners are rearrested within five years.[385]

DISARMED

Or look at the gang problem in the United States. According to the latest FBI data, the U.S. has about 1.4 million gang members spread across thirty-three thousand gangs.[386] In fewer than fifteen years, the number of gang members doubled and the number of gangs increased by more than 60 percent.[387] Gangs account for nearly half of all violent crime in the United States, according to the National Gang Center.[388] That includes about 13 percent of homicides.[389] Incidentally, when you hear statistics about the frequency of "mass shootings," you're usually hearing a figure that includes turf wars between rival gangs and crimes like armed robberies gone bad, not to mention domestic-violence incidents.[390] That's not to diminish the seriousness of those problems. It's simply to say that when you hear the term "mass shooting," you probably don't think immediately of gang wars. You're more likely to picture a madman going to a school or some other public place and gunning people down. A single "mass shooting" statistic that lumps together everything from gang wars to domestic violence to robberies misleads people and stokes fear.

Gangs terrorize and tyrannize people from coast to coast. Some 86 percent of U.S. cities with populations above one hundred thousand report gang problems.[391] But you'll even find gangs in small cities and rural areas.[392] In California, for example, the infamous MS-13 gang—for which the FBI created a national task force in 2004[393]—has invaded everything from small farming communities to the state's largest city.[394] In New York, the U.S. Attorney said, "MS-13 is responsible for a wave of death and violence that has terrorized communities, leaving neighborhoods on Long Island and throughout the Eastern District of New York awash in bloodshed."[395] MS-13 is active in many other places, including Massachusetts, Ohio, Texas, New Jersey, Maryland, Georgia, North Carolina, and Virginia.[396]

Or consider the surge in illegal border crossings into America. In 2022, Border Patrol agents caught more than 2.4 million people trying to break through the southern border. That's more than *five times* as many as in 2020.[397] The number of crimes committed by illegal migrants has skyrocketed as well. In 2022, illegal migrants were convicted of more than twelve thousand crimes, a nearly 500 percent increase over 2020's total. Homicides, murders, assaults, sexual offenses, drug trafficking—all these crimes and more jumped.[398]

Or think back to the growing risks discussed in the opening chapter, including the rise in polarization and political violence that has more than a third of Americans concerned about a civil war.[399]

Then throw in the possibility of an economic collapse, which would surely bring chaos and violence. That might seem unlikely to you. But, nearly half of Americans fear that a "total economic collapse" is coming.[400] And we recently woke up to some of the largest bank failures in American history with the demise of the Silicon Valley Bank and Signature Bank.[401] Overseas, just look at Venezuela to see how fast a nation's fortunes can change. As late as 2012, Venezuela was the richest country in South America, with the world's largest oil reserves. GDP soared year after year. Only a decade later, the oil reserves remained, but the country was in shambles, beset by hyperinflation, violence, corruption, and an incompetent, free-spending authoritarian government.[402]

The point is, tyranny and terror come in many forms—and most of the time, neither the police nor the army will be able to protect you. But you can protect yourself through armed self-defense.

What will happen, though, if the anti-gun lobby keeps eviscerating your right to keep and bear arms? You'll be left vulnerable. All of us will be.

All of us, that is, except for the politicians, celebrities, and billionaires who crusade for gun control. Many of them enjoy armed guards and 24/7 security.

Whether they admit it to themselves or not, these people trying to take away gun rights from others recognize the importance of armed self-defense. They especially understand the deterrent effect. After all, the Secret Service protecting President Joe Biden, and the U.S. Capitol Police protecting anti-gun senators and representatives aren't looking to get into a gunfight with armed attackers, kidnappers, and the like. Their first objective is to *deter* such attacks.

The same applies to prominent anti-gun crusaders outside of Washington. Consider Michael Bloomberg, the former New York City mayor who has poured millions into bankrolling gun-control causes. Bloomberg surrounds himself with armed security.[403] Whenever Bloomberg traveled to gun-free Bermuda—which was a lot—he'd bring armed guards with him. What's so strange about that?

Bermuda has outlawed guns; even most police don't carry them.[404] By the anti-gunners' logic, shouldn't Bermuda be the safest place in the world? Shouldn't Bloomberg feel safe to go there without guns? Oh, but wait, I guess gun control applies only to "We the little people."

Or take Facebook founder Mark Zuckerberg. Zuckerberg tends to keep mum on political issues, but even he has come out for gun control.[405] Facebook prohibits ads that "promote the sale or use of weapons, ammunition, or explosives."[406] But do you know how much Meta (Facebook's parent company) spent on security for Zuckerberg in 2021? Nearly $27 million. That's more than $70,000 *per day*. With that comes 24/7 protection by bodyguards. Do you think at that price it brings with it a few guns? The *San Francisco Chronicle* reported that Zuckerberg's San Francisco home is "under 24-hour surveillance by a team of about 15 guards on rotating shifts."[407] And that's just one of more than a dozen homes Zuckerberg owns.[408]

The rest of us aren't so lucky. We need our own guns to defend ourselves and our communities.

You know who really benefits from gun bans? Criminals, because they simply ignore the laws.

The prominent Italian thinker Cesare Beccaria made this point back in the eighteenth century.[409] Beccaria is known as the father of modern criminology.[410] He significantly influenced America's Founders. John Adams and Thomas Jefferson were so taken with his work that they copied passages from it by hand. James Madison included Beccaria in his list of recommended reading for the Continental Congress.[411] The great British attorney William Blackstone, a seminal influence on the Founders, cited Beccaria more than any other source in his famous *Commentaries*.[412]

In a passage that Jefferson copied into his personal quotation book, Beccaria wrote that gun bans disarm only those "who are not disposed to commit the crime which the laws mean to prevent."[413] In other words, only law-abiding citizens will comply with the laws.

Writing of violent criminals, Beccaria asked, "Can it be supposed, that those who have the courage to violate the most sacred laws of humanity, and the most important of the code, will respect the less considerable and arbitrary injunctions, the violation of which is so easy, and of so little comparative importance?"[414]

Beccaria's point has come down to us in simpler terms: *if guns are outlawed, only outlaws will have guns.*

Beccaria concluded that gun restrictions have the perverse effect of making law-abiding citizens less safe. Any such law, he wrote, "makes the situation of the assaulted worse, and of the assailants better, and rather encourages than prevents murder, as it requires less courage to attack unarmed than armed persons."[415]

Jefferson wrote "false ideas of utility" in the margin next to this part of Beccaria's passage: "For example, that legislator has false ideas of utility, who considers particular more than general convenience... who would sacrifice a thousand real advantages, to the fear of an imaginary or trifling inconvenience; who would deprive men of the use of fire, for fear of being burnt, and of water, for fear of being drowned."[416]

Cesare Beccaria helped to inspire America's Founders to enshrine the right to keep and bear arms. And he anticipated—and condemned—the "public safety" arguments that the anti-gun crowd uses to justify restrictions on your Second Amendment rights.

Learn from Ukraine. Learn from history. Don't let anyone rob you of your ability to defend your life and liberty.

6

THE DOOMSDAY PROVISION

Ukrainians now understand a point that too many Americans don't—that an armed citizenry is essential because it offers the best last resort against tyranny and terror of all kinds. Ukraine's leaders wouldn't hand out guns to civilians and call on them to make Molotov cocktails if they didn't understand this point.

In Chapter 3, I mentioned a Ukrainian attorney who, on the eve of the Russian invasion, said, "We always look at the Second Amendment of the U.S. Constitution." That lawyer added an important point. He said: "It is not just about self-protection, but the protection of freedom and the protection of independence. We Ukrainians really show this meaning of the Second Amendment."[417]

He's absolutely right. The right to keep and bear arms is fundamental to protecting liberty and independence.

Americans *used to* understand this point. Many still do, particularly the millions who exercise their Second Amendment rights with the AR-15 and like rifles, which have aptly been called "America's Rifle."[418]

Liberty and Independence

Founding Father Patrick Henry was talking about this very point in his "Give me liberty or give me death" speech. Do you remember the context of that famous address? It was March 1775, less than a month before the American Revolution began. Henry was urging his fellow Virginians to prepare—to organize armed volunteers to defend their home. He said this was "nothing less than a question of freedom or slavery." Henry also reminded his audience that "the battle…is not to the strong alone; it is to the vigilant, the active, the brave."[419]

The people of Ukraine heeded Patrick Henry's message and showed how much wisdom it contains.

Henry made another point in the same speech. He said, "Three millions of people, armed in the holy cause of liberty, and in such a country as that which we possess, are invincible by any force which our enemy can send against us."[420]

Some of Henry's contemporaries surely scoffed at the idea that the Americans could defeat the mighty British military. I'm sure King George III scoffed. Just like the gun-control crusaders today dismiss the usefulness of an armed citizenry. But Henry was right then, and the gun controllers are wrong now. As this book has shown, armed civilians have repeatedly helped to disrupt and even to defeat powerful militaries.

Noah Webster is best remembered for producing the first American dictionary. But he was also a prominent champion of the U.S. Constitution. In 1787, he wrote a pro-ratification pamphlet in which he said: "Before a standing army can rule, the people must be disarmed; as they are in almost every kingdom in Europe. The supreme power in America cannot enforce unjust laws by the sword; because the whole body of the people are armed, and constitute a force superior to any band of regular troops that can be, on any pretence, raised in the United States."[421]

Webster's point is similar to one Justice Joseph Story made several decades later. Recall that Story said the militia—that is, the people—represented "the natural defence of a free country against sudden foreign invasions, domestic insurrections, and domestic usurpations of power by rulers." That's why Story called the right to keep and bear arms "the palladium of the liberties of a republic."[422]

That's also why America's Founders passed laws requiring able-bodied male citizens to enroll in the militia, and to supply their own privately owned arms and ammunition. The Founders saw armed preparedness and private weapons as the defense of liberty.

Do you remember the Virginia law discussed in Chapter 4, the one designed for "Regulating and Disciplining the Militia, and Guarding Against Invasions and Insurrections"? The first line of the act clearly stated its foundational premise: "the defence and safety of the commonwealth depend upon having its citizens properly armed and taught the knowledge of military duty."[423]

That's a truth that Finland, Switzerland, Estonia, Latvia, and Lithuania have recognized but that Ukraine dismissed for too long.

The key question is, will the gun-control movement, blue-state governments bent on "massive resistance" to Supreme Court decisions,[424] and ruling-class national figures like Joe "F-15" Biden convince—or coerce—enough Americans to surrender their right to keep and bear arms? Will the United States forget the importance of an armed citizenry?

Denying Freedom

The right to possess arms marks an important difference between a free person and a slave, between a citizen and a serf.

Andrew Fletcher made this point in the late seventeenth century. Fletcher was a Scottish patriot and advocate of militias whose works influenced Thomas Jefferson. He used the phrase "well-regulated militia" that was later included in the Second Amendment. In his book *A Discourse of Government with Relation to Militias* (1698), Fletcher wrote, "I cannot see why arms should be denied to any man who is not a slave, since they are the only true badges of liberty… neither can I understand why any man that has arms should not be taught the use of them."[425]

DISARMED

Americans think of the right to arms as a birthright under the U.S. Constitution, as part of their essential freedoms. Yet disarmament is an often-overlooked element of America's shameful history of slavery and racial discrimination. Slaves were (for the most part) disarmed in colonial and antebellum times. Alain Stephens, a reporter for the anti-gun news outlet *The Trace*,[426] told NPR that Bacon's Rebellion, a 1676 uprising in Virginia in which black slaves aligned with white indentured servants, prompted the government to "roll out slave laws." One component of those slave laws, Stephens said, "ensured that Black people, whether they were enslaved or free, were not able to get firearms." Whenever other rebellions occurred, "the government would step down hard and fast to further racially stratify the [gun] laws."[427]

In the infamous *Dred Scott* decision (1857), the Supreme Court recoiled from recognizing free persons of color as citizens. Why? Chief Justice Roger Taney wrote that to do so would give Black people fundamental rights, including the right to "keep and carry arms wherever they went."[428]

Until ratification of the Fourteenth Amendment in 1868, the Southern slave codes ensured that African Americans had no rights under the First and Second Amendments, or any other part of the Bill of Rights. The defect at the Founding was that the basic rights of African Americans were not recognized. Rights like free speech and bearing arms were not adopted in support of slavery. Instead these rights were explicitly guaranteed to "the people," without distinction of color. It took the abolition of slavery to bring that to pass.[429]

You might expect the situation to have changed after the Civil War, when the Thirteenth, Fourteenth, and Fifteenth Amendments abolished slavery and guaranteed Black Americans the full rights of citizenship. But no. Southern state and local governments almost immediately instituted "Black Codes," many of which kept Black Americans from having guns.[430] For example, Alabama prohibited "any freedman, mulatto or free person of color in this state, [from owning] firearms, or carry[ing] about his person a pistol or other deadly weapon."[431] Mississippi decreed that no freedman "shall keep or carry fire-arms of any kind, or any ammunition" without police permission.[432]

Frederick Douglass understood that the right to arms is crucial for freedom. In 1863, the former-slave-turned-prominent-abolitionist asked, "Shall we be wholly free, an equal at the ballot-box, at the jury-box, and at the cartridge-box, with the white man?"[433] Years later, in his autobiography, Douglass recalled that he saw "no chance of bettering the condition of the freedman until he should cease to be merely a freedman and should become a citizen." A citizen needed the liberties of "the ballot-box, the jury-box, and the cartridge-box," without which "no class of people could live and flourish in this country."[434]

Douglass and countless other civil rights leaders fought for the right that offered the ultimate protection of freedom. Nearly a century after Douglass, Martin Luther King Jr. chafed at a system that denied him his right to bear arms and protect himself and his family. In 1956, King's home in Montgomery, Alabama, was bombed. In response, King applied for a gun-carry permit. At the time, Alabama law allowed government officials to deny people permits to carry firearms outside the home. (This is the kind of discretionary law that the Supreme Court struck down in 2022 in *New York State Rifle and Pistol Association v. Bruen*.)[435] The local sheriff turned King down.

Telling fellow protest organizers about the sheriff's decision, King concluded, "In substance he was saying, 'You are at the disposal of the hoodlums.'"[436]

Today's gun prohibitionists want to leave you at the disposal of the hoodlums—and of violent criminals, psychopaths, terrorists, and tyrants. In the name of "public safety," they want you to accept all kinds of restrictions on your right to keep and bear arms. In their ideal scenario, you wouldn't have any guns at all.

Unless you want to be caught unprepared and defenseless, don't let them trample on your constitutional right to armed self-defense.

Surprise Happens

Tyranny and terror come in many different forms. But let's return to the scenario that Ukraine is enduring. Let's return to those Black Swan events we discussed in the opening chapter—the sorts of "we never saw it coming" developments that recur throughout history.

Even Russia's invasion of Ukraine qualifies. The invasion shouldn't have caught the Ukrainians off guard, given Russia's long history of trying to take (or take back) Ukraine and especially Putin's aggressive stance. And, yet, it *did* catch them off guard. In the weeks leading up to the invasion, President Volodymyr Zelenskyy repeatedly told the Ukrainian people not to panic.[437] You could chalk those comments up to public posturing and trying to avoid destabilizing his country. But even in private, Zelenskyy expressed skepticism that Russia would invade.[438] Much of the international community felt the same way.[439]

They were all wrong.

So, remember, when you hear your fellow Americans say, "It can't happen here," they could be wrong too. And if they are wrong, do you want to be scrambling in desperation the way so many Ukrainians were?

True enough, the chances of a foreign invasion of the United States seem small today. But small is not the same as nonexistent. And "today" inevitably gives way to a tomorrow and to the future.

People tend to forget that there have been attacks on U.S. territory throughout our history. Most obviously, British troops and mercenaries were sent to the newly independent states for years during the Revolutionary War. The British claimed they were suppressing a rebellion, but the Americans won the war. So, in hindsight that was an invasion of the U.S. mainland by foreign troops.

DISARMED

In the War of 1812, the British occupied and burned Washington, D.C., and bombarded Fort McHenry in Maryland.[440] They invaded Louisiana, lost a pitched battle outside of New Orleans, and ultimately retreated.[441]

Prior to the outbreak of the Mexican-American War, the boundary between the United States and Mexico was disputed. The Americans claimed that the Rio Grande was the boundary, and the Mexicans asserted that the boundary was the Nueces River farther north. A small American force stationed along the Rio Grande was attacked by a much larger force from the Mexican army sent across the Rio Grande, and nearly all of the Americans were killed or captured, prompting the war. Since the boundary was later settled as the Rio Grande, this was an invasion of the U.S. mainland, and was treated as such by President Polk and Congress at the time.[442]

In the U.S. Civil War, the North considered the seceded states to be in a state of rebellion and did not recognize the Confederacy as a nation-state. That was similar to the situation with the British in the Revolutionary War, but this time the previous government prevailed in the war (unlike the British). Many historians would claim that the Confederacy was not invaded because the Confederacy had no legal existence. To the South, however, which had functioning national and state governments, it seemed like an invasion. If the territory of the Confederacy was not considered sovereign, but remained part of the United States, it may be said that a large part of the United States was invaded by the United States Army, which wreaked destruction until that part surrendered and was placed under military occupation.

Around the beginning of World War I, Pancho Villa attacked an American town in New Mexico, killing seventeen Americans. Although he had just led a successful revolution in Mexico, he had been displaced from power and conducted the raid to try to get the United States to declare war on Mexico. So, he didn't represent a nation-state, but did lead a group of Mexicans in a political attack on American mainland soil. The United States sent an army into Mexico under General John Pershing to try to capture him, but that effort was unsuccessful.[443]

In World War I, at a time when America had not yet entered the war, a German sabotage ring blew up a major munitions' storage depot at Black Tom Island in Jersey City, New Jersey. It "exploded with a massive blast felt for a hundred miles, blowing out most of the windows in lower Manhattan, damaging the Statue of Liberty…killing at least four people, and injuring hundreds as 2,000,000 pounds of small arms and artillery ammunition and 100,000 pounds of TNT detonated…." The munitions were destined for shipment to Russia, which was why the Germans blew them up. After America entered the war, the ring also "conducted another spectacular sabotage attack in the United States, when, on the morning of 9 July 1917, a massive blast rocked the Mare Island Shipyard and numerous barges filled with munitions, killing six, wounding 31, and causing damage across a wide area of northern San Francisco Bay."[444]

DISARMED

The Japanese, of course, bombed Pearl Harbor in December 1941. It was a U.S. territory at the time, not a state, and was far removed from the mainland. But we all know the reaction it provoked.

In World War II, nine Japanese submarines also briefly tried attacking U.S. commercial shipping off the Pacific Coast. For the most part the attacks were unsuccessful, although two merchant ships were sunk, several damaged, and six merchant seamen were killed.[445] One sub shelled an oil field in California, with little damage. Another sub attacked an American fort on the Oregon coastline, firing a number of artillery shells from its 140 mm deck gun.[446] There was only minor damage to the fort. In the fall of 1942, a Japanese sub released a float plane that bombed a forest in Oregon with incendiary bombs, with little effect. A second such raid was carried out a couple of weeks later.[447]

In June of 1942, the Japanese also occupied two islands in the Aleutians, which was then U.S. territory but not a state. In May of 1943, the U.S. sent troops to reclaim those islands, and a fierce eighteen-day battle was fought on the island of Attu. That was the only battle in the Aleutians, and the Japanese were nearly wiped out through battle deaths, bitterly cold weather, and suicides.[448] Late in the war, the Japanese released thousands of fire balloons to drift across the Pacific, hoping to ignite major fires in the American West. One of these succeeded in killing a pregnant woman and five children on an outing in the woods.[449]

The 9/11 attacks took place on the American mainland. Although not carried out directly by a nation-state, fifteen of the nineteen attackers were Saudi Arabian nationals.[450]

America has sustained a continuing, illegal invasion of people from Latin America across the U.S-Mexican border for over a decade, often encouraged by the U.S. government. It has been aided and abetted by nation-states in Latin America.

In any case, foreign invasion is far from the only form of tyranny we may confront. Mark Cancian, an expert at the Center for Strategic and International Studies, has chronicled the surprise factor in warfare. By "surprise," he doesn't refer narrowly to surprise attacks like Japan's raid on Pearl Harbor or 9/11. He means any events "that so contravene the victim's expectations that opponents gain a major advantage."[451] After reviewing the long history of surprises in war, Cancian concludes that we can't avoid surprise but can do our best to prepare and learn how to cope with it when it occurs. "Surprise happens," he writes. "There will be a next time."[452]

And yes, that includes America. Cancian writes that the United States confronts "huge, often unacknowledged, uncertainties," and "in these uncertainties lies the possibility of surprise." He identifies factors that make the United States "particularly vulnerable today": the rise of China and Russia as competing great powers, the false sense of perpetual security that has come from the "long peace between great powers," and "changes in warfighting technology that have transformed the conduct of battle since the last great power conflict."[453]

Cancian isn't saying that China will invade the American homeland tomorrow. The Chinese probably won't invade, especially because, as we saw in the first chapter, they could cause chaos and destruction in the United States without putting soldiers on American soil. Cancian thinks it's hubris to think "it can't happen here." So, we need to stand ready for any surprises that may lurk.

It Can Happen Anywhere

You and I can't control how the U.S. military prepares for surprises. But we can control how *we* prepare. That means learning from Ukraine's mistakes so that we don't repeat them.

Ukraine never protected the right to keep and bear arms; powerful forces in the United States are working actively to deprive people of that fundamental civil right, even though it stands as "the palladium of the liberties of a republic."

Ukraine waited until the last minute to allow its citizens to carry firearms outside the home; states like New York and California are doing their best to take away what the Supreme Court has affirmed is a *constitutional* right to carry.

Ukraine left its citizens scrambling to buy guns and learn how to use them; the anti-gun lobby in the United States wants to ban whole classes of civilian firearms, and then prevent ordinary Americans from possessing or using any private firearms that remain legal.

Ukraine destroyed its weapons stockpile, leaving civilians so desperate for guns and training that they practiced with plywood cutouts in the shape of rifles; the ultimate goal of anti-gunners in the United States is to have all of us turn in our guns—you know, disarm ourselves.[454]

But it's up to us to preserve the right to keep and bear arms, which is crucial to protecting liberty and independence.

Even *The New Yorker*—not what you'd call a champion of gun rights—confessed to having second thoughts based on Ukraine's experience. A *New Yorker* reporter had to acknowledge that what he saw on the ground early in the war challenged his assumptions about armed civilians. Describing members of a civilian sniper club he met, the reporter wrote: "I recognized these men. Of course, the difference between them and their American analogues—preppers, survivalists, militia members—was that the dreaded scenario they had envisaged was not a lurid fantasy."[455]

Then the reporter recounted meeting a Ukrainian who had lived in Alberta, Canada, before returning to his homeland to join in the defense. The man, code-named "Canada," had served in Ukraine's Donbas region in 2016. He had participated in a counteroffensive against pro-Russian separatists there who wanted to secede. Canada told the reporter that the lesson he drew from his Donbas tour was "It can happen anywhere." So, once he settled in Alberta, he stocked up on guns and ammunition. (He did all this before Canadian prime minister Justin Trudeau began trampling on gun rights by, for example, banning more than 1,500 kinds of so-called "assault weapons" and putting a freeze on the sale of all handguns.)[456]

The *New Yorker* reporter commented: "Had we met in North America, I likely would have seen Canada's world view as paranoid and apocalyptic. In Ukraine, though, it was harder to dismiss."[457]

But why should anyone "dismiss" the idea of being prepared to protect yourself, your home, your family, your community, and your country? Without private gun ownership, people are defenseless in the face of tyrants, gangs, criminals, and other threats. If you doubt that, remember to ask yourself, why has virtually every mass-murdering tyrant in history tried to disarm the people?

Or think again of the words of George Packer. Packer has reported on wars before. He also won the National Book Award for *The Unwinding*, which depicted Americans coming apart and beset by crisis. Yet even he did not understand the stakes until he saw Ukrainian civilians fighting to save their homeland. Remember what Packer wrote? "It almost seemed as if the U.S. would have to be attacked or undergo some other catastrophe for Americans to remember what Ukrainians have known from the start."[458]

But if you wait until catastrophe comes, it's too late. That's why I've written this book. I want to do everything possible to make sure that Americans don't allow the right that the Founders enshrined—to keep and bear arms—to become a nullity, only a remembrance of the freedom and protections we once had. As I've said, it's good to learn from your own mistakes, but it's so much better to learn from other people's mistakes. Ukraine made several mistakes we can learn from—*if* we bother to pay attention.

The Bitter Lessons of History

Ukraine's experience with the Russian invasion underscores retired federal judge Alex Kozinski's brilliant analysis in a Second Amendment case. Kozinski knows what he is talking about. His father spent four years in a concentration camp, and his mother spent World War II in a Jewish ghetto. He and his family emigrated from Communist Romania to this country when he was twelve. In a blistering dissenting opinion, Judge Kozinski wrote:

> *All too many of the other great tragedies of history—Stalin's atrocities, the killing fields of Cambodia, the Holocaust, to name but a few—were perpetrated by armed troops against unarmed populations. Many could well have been avoided or mitigated, had the perpetrators known their intended victims were equipped with a rifle and twenty bullets apiece, as the Militia Act required here [in the United States].*[459]

Judge Kozinski warned that those who want to trample on the Second Amendment "have forgotten these bitter lessons of history." He continued:

DISARMED

> *The prospect of tyranny may not grab the headlines the way vivid stories of gun crime routinely do. But few saw the Third Reich coming until it was too late. The Second Amendment is a doomsday provision, one designed for those exceptionally rare circumstances where all other rights have failed—where the government refuses to stand for reelection and silences those who protest; where courts have lost the courage to oppose, or can find no one to enforce their decrees.*[460]

Yes, Judge Kozinski said, such contingencies may seem "improbable" today. But he concluded with a warning we must never forget: "facing them unprepared is a mistake a free people get to make only once."[461]

ENDNOTES

[1] See, e.g., John Paul Stevens, "Repeal the Second Amendment," *New York Times*, March 27, 2018, https://www.nytimes.com/2018/03/27/opinion/john-paul-stevens-repeal-second-amendment.html ("...a relic of the 18th century); "The Second Amendment," Giffords Law Center to Prevent Gun Violence, https://giffords.org/lawcenter/gun-laws/second-amendment/ ("We no longer rely on civilian militias as a form of national defense.... For almost two centuries, the majority of Americans viewed the Second Amendment as a relic of these militias"); Duncan Hosie, "Gun-Rights Activists Remade the Second Amendment Over Past 40 Years," *Washington Post*, June 3, 2022, https://www.washingtonpost.com/outlook/2022/06/03/gun-rights-activists-remade-2nd-amendment-over-last-40-years/ ("Liberals decry the amendment as a dangerous relic; some even call for its repeal"); Roger Sollenberger, "Repeal the Second Amendment, Idiots," *Paste*, March 30, 2018, https://www.pastemagazine.

com/politics/gun-control/repeal-the-second-amendment-idiots/ (I mean, you can probably guess the tone from the headline, but here's a representative quotation just in case: "The Second Amendment truly is a relic.... We should all at least agree the Second Amendment is antiquated").

2 Luke Harding, "Business Brisk at Kyiv Gun Shops as Ukrainians Rush to Buy Arms," *The Guardian* (UK), February 23, 2022, https://www.theguardian.com/world/2022/feb/23/business-brisk-at-kyiv-gun-shops-as-ukrainians-rush-to-buy-arms.

3 Stephen P. Halbrook, America's Rifle: The Case for the AR-15 (Post-Hill Press 2022).

4 Azmi Haroun, "Ukraine's Parliament Passed a Law Allowing Citizens to Carry Firearms, and a Local NGO Official Said 'There's a Feeling That Ukrainians Will Fight,'" *Business Insider*, February 23, 2022, https://www.businessinsider.com/ukraine-parliament-passes-law-allowing-citizens-to-carry-firearms-2022-2.

5 Isabelle Khurshudyan, Siobhán O'Grady, and Loveday Morris, "'Weapons to Anyone': Across Ukraine, Militias Form as Russian Forces Near," *Washington Post*, February 26, 2022, https://www.washingtonpost.com/world/2022/02/26/ukraine-russia-militias/.

6 "Ukrainian Woman, 79, Takes Part in Military Training in Case Russia Invades Ukraine," Sky News, February 14, 2022, https://news.sky.com/story/

ukrainian-woman-79-takes-part-in-military-training-in-case-russia-invades-ukraine-12542002.

7   Luke Mogelson, "How Ukrainians Saved Their Capital," *New Yorker*, May 2, 2022, https://www.newyorker.com/magazine/2022/05/09/how-ukrainians-saved-their-capital; "Ukrainian Civilians Continue to Fight for Their Country," *NBC Nightly News*, February 26, 2022, https://www.nbcnews.com/nightly-news/video/ukrainian-civilians-continue-to-fight-for-their-country-134134341791; Andrew E. Kramer, "'Everybody in Our Country Needs to Defend,'" *New York Times*, February 26, 2022, https://www.nytimes.com/2022/02/26/world/europe/ukraine-russia-civilian-military.html; Christina Olha Jarymowycz, "POV: Ukrainian Civilians Are Flipping the Script of Warfare," *BU Today*, March 15, 2022, https://www.bu.edu/articles/2022/pov-ukrainian-civilians-are-flipping-the-script-of-warfare/.

8   Jacqui Heinrich and Adam Sabes, "Gen. Milley Says Kyiv Could Fall Within 72 hours If Russia Decides to Invade Ukraine: Sources," Fox News, February 5, 2022, https://www.foxnews.com/us/gen-milley-says-kyiv-could-fall-within-72-hours-if-russia-decides-to-invade-ukraine-sources.

9   Lindsay Kornick, "Biden Blasted for Mocking 'Brave' Second Amendment Defenders: 'You Need an F-15' to Fight America, Not a Gun," Fox News, August 30, 2022, https://www.foxnews.com/media/biden-blasted-mocking-brave-second-amendment-defenders-you-need-f-15-fight-america-not-gun.

10. Geoffrey Skelley, "Why Eric Swalwell's Campaign Failed," FiveThirtyEight, July 8, 2019, https://fivethirtyeight.com/features/why-eric-swalwells-campaign-failed/.
11. Eric Swalwell, "Ban Assault Weapons, Buy Them Back, Go After Resisters," *USA Today*, May 3, 2018, https://www.usatoday.com/story/opinion/2018/05/03/ban-assault-weapons-buy-them-back-prosecute-offenders-column/570590002/.
12. Eric Swalwell, Twitter, November 16, 2018, https://twitter.com/RepSwalwell/status/1063527635114852352.
13. James Marson, "The Ragtag Army That Won the Battle of Kyiv and Saved Ukraine," *Wall Street Journal*, September 20, 2022, https://www.wsj.com/articles/russian-invasion-ukraine-battle-of-kyiv-ragtag-army-11663683336; Olga Tokariuk, "How Ukrainian Citizens Are Mobilizing to Provide Aid and Supplies in the Fight Against Russia," *Time*, March 11, 2022, https://time.com/6156886/ukrainian-citizens-mobilizing-against-russia/; Mogelson, "How Ukrainians Saved Their Capital."
14. Anthony Constantini, "Analysis: What Ukraine's Embrace of Gun Rights as Russia Attacks Could Mean for Europe," *The Reload*, February 23, 2022, https://thereload.com/analysis-ukraines-embrace-of-the-right-to-national-self-defense/.
15. Isabel van Brugen, "Ukraine Citizen Who 'Destroyed' Russian Su-34 Jet with Rifle Given Medal," *Newsweek*, August 19, 2022, https://www.newsweek.com/ukraine-citizen-russian-su-34-fighter-jet-rifle-medal-1735169.

16 Harding, "Business Brisk at Kyiv Gun Shops as Ukrainians Rush to Buy Arms."

17 Shaun Walker and Andrew Roth, "'They Took Our Clothes': Ukrainians Returning to Looted Homes," *The Guardian* (UK), April 11, 2022, https://www.theguardian.com/world/2022/apr/11/ukrainian-homes-looted-by-russian-soldiers; Zoe Strozewski, "Russian Soldiers Looting in Ukraine May Also Be Stealing From Putin: Report," *Newsweek*, May 26, 2022, https://www.newsweek.com/russian-soldiers-looting-ukraine-may-also-stealing-putin-report-1710533.

18 Kim Bubello and Chad de Guzman, "'We Are Fighting for Survival': The Ukrainian Citizens Volunteering to Defend Their Country from Russian Troops," *Time*, March 3, 2022, https://time.com/6154068/ukrainian-citizens-fight-russian-troops/; Liz Cookman, "Ukraine's Civilian Militia Trains to Protect Kiev from Russia," *The National*, January 31, 2022, https://www.thenationalnews.com/world/europe/2022/01/31/ukraines-civilian-militia-trains-to-protect-kiev-from-russia/.

19 Harding, "Business Brisk at Kyiv Gun Shops as Ukrainians Rush to Buy Arms."

20 Cookman, "Ukraine's Civilian Militia Trains to Protect Kiev from Russia."

21 Josh Lederman and Ed Flanagan, "Ukraine's Soldiers Have Rockets and Drones, but Are Running Low in Boots and T-Shirts," NBC News, August 20, 2022, https://www.nbcnews.com/news/world/

ukraines-soldiers-rockets-drones-are-running-low-boots-t-shirts-rcna43902; Jeffrey Gettleman, "In Ukraine's South, Fierce Fighting and Deadly Costs," *New York Times*, September 24, 2022, https://www.nytimes.com/2022/09/24/world/europe/ukraine-south-kherson-russia.html.

22 See, e.g., Cookman, "Ukraine's Civilian Militia Trains to Protect Kiev from Russia"; Trudy Rubin, "Ukrainian Civilians Train for War with Cardboard Guns: 'We Are Scared but We Are Ready,'" *Philadelphia Inquirer*, February 7, 2022, https://www.inquirer.com/opinion/ukraine-russia-military-training-civilians-20220207.html; Liam Collins and John Spencer, "How Volunteers Can Help Defeat Great Powers," *Military Times*, July 5, 2022, https://www.militarytimes.com/opinion/commentary/2022/07/05/how-volunteers-can-defeat-great-powers/. This Reuters piece rounds up a number of news outlets that covered the cutout guns: Reuters Fact Check, "Fact Check: Image of Individuals with Wooden Guns in Ukraine Was Taken at Training Exercises Prior to Russian Invasion," Reuters, March 1, 2022, https://www.reuters.com/article/factcheck-ukraine-wooden-guns/fact-check-image-of-individuals-with-wooden-guns-in-ukraine-was-taken-at-training-exercises-prior-to-russian-invasion-idUSL1N2V42K9. To be fair, there is a long history of using dummy training weapons. After the surprise attack on Pearl Harbor, for example, the U.S. military found itself so short of weapons that it placed a rush order for dummy training rifles. The point is, though,

that you never want to be caught with the kind of arms shortfall situation Ukraine was. That could happen in the United States if gun prohibitionists succeed in taking away firearms and gun rights. Elyssa Vondra (Jackson), "A Training Rifle-Maker Who Is No Dummy," U.S. Army, https://www.army.mil/article/216837/a_training_rifle_maker_who_is_no_dummy.

23 Graeme Wood, "How the Finns Deter Russian Invasion," *The Atlantic*, March 2, 2022, https://www.theatlantic.com/ideas/archive/2022/03/finlands-model-resisting-russian-aggression/623334/.

24 Max Boot, "To Deter a Russian Attack, Ukraine Needs to Prepare for Guerrilla Warfare," *Washington Post*, December 15, 2021, https://www.washingtonpost.com/opinions/2021/12/15/ukraine-russia-putin-aggression-nato/.

25 See, e.g., Bureau of Political-Military Affairs, "Fact Sheet: U.S. Security Cooperation with Ukraine," U.S. Department of State, September 8, 2022, https://www.state.gov/u-s-security-cooperation-with-ukraine/; "Fact Sheet on U.S. Security Assistance for Ukraine," White House, March 16, 2022, https://www.whitehouse.gov/briefing-room/statements-releases/2022/03/16/fact-sheet-on-u-s-security-assistance-for-ukraine/; Jordan Cohen, "Ukraine Receives Weapons Support from Around the World," The Conversation, May 6, 2022, https://theconversation.com/ukraine-receives-weapons-support-from-around-the-world-182266.

26 Amy Kazmin, Benjamin Parkin, and Katrina Manson, "Low Morale, No Support, and Bad Politics: Why the Afghan Army Folded," *Financial Times*, August 15, 2021, https://www.ft.com/content/b1d2b06d-f938-4443-ba56-242f18da22c3.

27 "Remarks by President Biden on Afghanistan," White House, August 16, 2021, https://www.whitehouse.gov/briefing-room/speeches-remarks/2021/08/16/remarks-by-president-biden-on-afghanistan/.

28 Kazmin, Parkin, and Manson, "Low Morale, No Support, and Bad Politics: Why the Afghan Army Folded."

29 Caleb Stark and John Stark, *Memoir and Official Correspondence of Gen. John Stark* (United States: G.P. Lyon, 1860). https://www.google.com/books/edition/Memoir_and_Official_Correspondence_of_Ge/DA1JarGdjicC?hl=en&gbpv=1&printsec=frontcover#v=onepage&q&f=false, and at https://sos.nh.gov/media/pyzjv3vq/memoir-of-general-john-stark-1860.pdf.

30 Tunku Varadarajan, "The Man Who Said Ukraine Would Win," *Wall Street Journal*, October 14, 2022, https://www.wsj.com/articles/the-man-who-said-ukraine-would-win-bernard-henri-levy-russia-putin-west-front-lines-america-strategy-paris-11665752884.

31 Duncan Ball, "7 Reasons Why America Could Never Be Invaded," Global Affairs Explained, undated, https://globalaffairsexplained.com/why-america-never-invaded/.

32. John Feng, "Three in 10 Americans Believe U.S. Will Be Invaded Within 10 Years: Poll," *Newsweek*, September 13, 2022, https://www.newsweek.com/yougov-poll-us-invasion-foreign-ministry-10-years-republicans-democrats-1742456.
33. Dennis E. Showalter and John Graham Royde-Smith, "World War I," *Encyclopedia Britannica*, January 18, 2023, https://www.britannica.com/event/World-War-I.
34. Nassim Nicholas Taleb, *The Black Swan: The Impact of the Highly Improbable*, 2nd ed. (New York: Random House, 2010), xxii.
35. Chandelis Duster, "Top Military Leader Says China's Hypersonic Missile Test 'Went Around the World,'" CNN, November 18, 2021, https://www.cnn.com/2021/11/17/politics/john-hyten-china-hypersonic-weapons-test.
36. Tara Copp, "'It Failed Miserably': After Wargaming Loss, Joint Chiefs Are Overhauling How the US Military Will Fight," Defense One, July 26, 2021, https://www.defenseone.com/policy/2021/07/it-failed-miserably-after-wargaming-loss-joint-chiefs-are-overhauling-how-us-military-will-fight/184050/.
37. "'The Big One Is Coming' and the U.S. Military Isn't Ready," *Wall Street Journal*, November 4, 2022, https://www.wsj.com/articles/the-big-one-is-coming-china-russia-charles-richard-u-s-military-11667597291.
38. Eduardo Baptista and Greg Torode, "Analysis: China's military has shown growing interest in high-altitude balloons," February 6, 2023, Reuters, https://www.reuters.com/world/china/chinas-

39 Chloe Folmar, "Large Majority Says They Are Concerned About Political Violence: Poll," *The Hill*, November 4, 2022, https://thehill.com/blogs/blog-briefing-room/3719384-large-majority-says-they-are-concerned-about-political-violence-poll/amp/.

40 Feng, "Three in 10 Americans Believe U.S. Will Be Invaded Within 10 Years: Poll."

41 Tim Malloy and Doug Schwartz, "Vast Majority of Americans Say Ban Russian Oil, Quinnipiac University National Poll Finds; Nearly 8 in 10 Support U.S. Military Response If Putin Attacks a NATO Country," Quinnipiac University Poll, March 7, 2022, https://poll.qu.edu/images/polling/us/us03072022_ujca44.pdf.

42 Joseph Story, *Commentaries on the Constitution* (1833), 3:§1890, https://press-pubs.uchicago.edu/founders/documents/amendIIs10.html. Story wrote that the "militia" provided this "national defence of a free country." But he wasn't talking about state-sponsored military organization like today's National Guard. As you'll see in Chapter 2, Story meant the people in general.

43 Bill Hutchinson and Patrick Reevell, "What Are the Ukraine 'Separatist' Regions at the Crux of the Russian Invasion," ABC News, March 4, 2022, https://abcnews.go.com/International/ukraine-separatist-regions-crux-russian-invasion/story?id=83084803.

44   Joe Concha, CNN ridiculed for 'Fiery But Mostly Peaceful' caption with video of burning building in Kenosha, 08/27/20, https://thehill.com/homenews/media/513902-cnn-ridiculed-for-fiery-but-mostly-peaceful-caption-with-video-of-burning/

45   Jemima McEvoy, "14 Days of Protests, 19 Dead," *Forbes*, June 8, 2020, https://www.forbes.com/sites/jemimamcevoy/2020/06/08/14-days-of-protests-19-dead/?sh=139598d54de4.

46   Ebony Bowden, "More Than 700 Officers Injured in George Floyd Protests Across US," *New York Post*, June 8, 2020, https://nypost.com/2020/06/08/more-than-700-officers-injured-in-george-floyd-protests-across-us/.

47   Jennifer A. Kingson, "Exclusive: $1 Billion-Plus Riot Damage Is Most Expensive in Insurance History," Axios, September 16, 2020, https://www.axios.com/riots-cost-property-damage-276c9bcc-a455-4067-b06a-66f9db4cea9c.html.

48   See, e.g., "Mayors of Major US Cities Reject Deployment of Federal Forces," VOA News, July 22, 2020, https://www.voanews.com/a/usa_race_america_mayors-major-us-cities-reject-deployment-federal-forces/6193218.html; see also Claudia Morell, "Chicago Mayor Asks Trump Not to Send Federal Agents, Saying It Would 'Spell Disaster,'" NPR, July 21, 2020, https://www.npr.org/local/309/2020/07/21/893466407/chicago-mayor-asks-trump-not-to-send-federal-agents-saying-it-would-spell-disaster.

49   Rosalina Nieves and Theresa Waldrop, "America Is on a Gun-Buying Spree. Here's What Is Driving

the Surge," CNN, June 4, 2021, https://www.cnn.com/2021/06/04/us/us-gun-sales-surge/index.html.

50 Shane Harris, Karen DeYoung, Isabelle Khurshudyan, Ashley Parker, and Liz Sly, "Road to War: U.S. Struggled to Convince Allies, and Zelensky, of Risk of Invasion," *Washington Post*, August 16, 2022, https://www.washingtonpost.com/national-security/interactive/2022/ukraine-road-to-war/.

51 Pam Greenberg and Matthew Sullivan, "Legislative Actions in Oversight of Executive Emergency Powers," National Conference of State Legislatures, last updated February 28, 2022, https://www.ncsl.org/research/about-state-legislatures/legislative-actions-in-oversight-of-executive-emergency-powers.aspx.

52 George Packer, *The Assassins' Gate: America in Iraq* (New York: Farrar, Straus and Giroux, 2005).

53 Nikhil Pal Singh, "Stuck in the Middle: George Packer's Liberal Faith," *The Nation*, November 15, 2021, https://www.thenation.com/article/politics/george-packer-last-best-hope/.

54 George Packer, "Ukrainians Are Defending the Values Americans Claim to Hold," *The Atlantic*, September 6, 2022, https://www.theatlantic.com/magazine/archive/2022/10/ukraine-invasion-civilian-volunteers-survival/671241/.

55 Packer, "Ukrainians Are Defending the Values Americans Claim to Hold."

56 Packer, "Ukrainians Are Defending the Values Americans Claim to Hold."

57 Packer, "Ukrainians Are Defending the Values Americans Claim to Hold."

58 Frank Langfitt, "On the 31st Anniversary of Ukraine's Split from Soviet Union, the War Hits Month 6," NPR, August 24, 2022, https://www.npr.org/2022/08/24/1119308512/on-the-31st-anniversary-of-ukraines-split-from-soviet-union-the-war-hits-month-6; Stephen P. Halbrook, "Ukraine War Reintroduces U.S. Politicians to the Second Amendment," *Washington Times*, March 29, 2022, https://www.washingtontimes.com/news/2022/mar/29/ukraine-war-reintroduces-us-politicians-to-the-sec/.

59 Constitution of Ukraine, Adopted at the Fifth Session of the Verkhovna Rada of Ukraine on June 28, 1996, Amended by the Laws of Ukraine № 2222-IV dated December 8, 2004, № 2952-VI dated February 1, 2011, № 586-VII dated September 19, 2013, № 742-VII dated February 21, 2014, № 1401-VIII dated June 2, 2016 № 2680-VIII dated February 7, 2019, https://www.refworld.org/pdfid/44a280124.pdf.

60 See Stephen P. Halbrook, Ph.D., Attorney at Law—Specializing in Constitutional Cases, https://stephenhalbrook.com/.

61 See "Joyce Lee Malcolm," Biographical Sketch, George Mason University: Antonin Scalia Law School, https://www.law.gmu.edu/faculty/directory/emeritus/malcolm_joyce.

62 *District of Columbia v. Heller*, 554 U.S. 570 (2008), https://supreme.justia.com/cases/federal/us/554/570/.

63 Stephen Halbrook, "The Right of the People to Keep and Bear Arms: The Second Amendment in the U.S. Bill of Rights," *Pravo Ukraine*, no. 2 (2013): 240-50, https://www.stephenhalbrook.com/wp-content/uploads/2022/03/Halbrook-Right-to-Bear-Arms-Ukranian-Law-Journal.pdf; Joyce Lee Malcolm, "Infringement," *Pravo Ukraine*, (2013), https://pravoua.com.ua/en/store/pravo_usa/usalaw_1-2_13/Malcolm-usa_2_13/. "Право народа на хранение и ношение оружия: вторая поправка билля о правах сша" ["The Right of the People to Keep and Bear Arms: the Second Amendment in the U.S. Bill of Rights"], 2 Ukrainian Law Journal "Law of the USA" (2013), 240-50. https://stephenhalbrook.com/wp-content/uploads/2022/03/%D0%9F%D1%80%D0%B0%D0%B2%D0%BE_%D0%A1%D0%A8%D0%90_-1-2_2013-Halbrook.pdf; "The Right of the People to Keep and Bear Arms: the Second Amendment in the U.S. Bill of Rights," 2 Ukrainian Law Journal "Law of the USA" (2013), 240-50. https://stephenhalbrook.com/wp-content/uploads/2022/03/Halbrook-Right-to-Bear-Arms-Ukranian-Law-Journal.pdf; Joyce Malcolm, "Обмеження прав" [Limitation of Rights], 2 Ukrainian Law Journal "Law of the USA" 251 (2013); see also Stephen P. Halbrook, "Ukraine War Reintroduces U.S. Politicians to the Second Amendment," Washington Times, March 29, 2022, https://www.washingtontimes.com/news/2022/mar/29/ukraine-war-reintroduces-us-politicians-to-the-sec/ ("In 2013, Ukraine's oldest law journal, the

Law of Ukraine, published an issue on the U.S. Bill of Rights. Having read my book, "The Founders' Second Amendment," the editor invited me to contribute an article on the subject. George Mason University Law Prof. Joyce Lee Malcolm, author of "To Keep and Bear Arms," also was featured.").

64 "Our History," *Pravo Ukraine*, https://pravoua.com.ua/en/our-history/.

65 "Ukrainian MPs Vote to Oust President Yanukovych," BBC News, February 22, 2014, https://www.bbc.com/news/world-europe-26304842.

66 Stephen P. Halbrook, "Ukraine War Reintroduces U.S. Politicians to the Second Amendment," Washington Times, March 29, 2022, https://www.washingtontimes.com/news/2022/mar/29/ukraine-war-reintroduces-us-politicians-to-the-sec/ /

67 Stephen P. Halbrook, "Ukraine War Reintroduces U.S. Politicians to the Second Amendment," Washington Times, March 29, 2022, https://www.washingtontimes.com/news/2022/mar/29/ukraine-war-reintroduces-us-politicians-to-the-sec/

68 See link found in Halbrook, "Ukraine War Reintroduces U.S. Politicians to the Second Amendment." "Ukraine War Reintroduces U.S. Politicians to the Second Amendment," Washington Times, March 29, 2022, https://www.washingtontimes.com/news/2022/mar/29/ukraine-war-reintroduces-us-politicians-to-the-sec/. When the link in the

Halbrook article is clicked, it goes to this article and webpage providing a translation of a proposed Ukrainian version of the Second Amendment. See Gun owners demand changes to the Constitution, 24.02.2014,| translation into English here https://zbroya-info.translate.goog/uk/blog/2675_vlasniki-zbroyi-vimagaiut-zmin-do-konstitutsiyi/?_x_tr_sl=auto&_x_tr_tl=en&_x_tr_hl=en (last checked March 12, 2023).

69 "About Association," Ukrainian Gun Owners Association, ZBROYA Info, https://zbroya.info/en/about/.

70 "The Crisis in Crimea and Eastern Ukraine," *Encyclopedia Britannica*, https://www.britannica.com/place/Ukraine/The-crisis-in-Crimea-and-eastern-Ukraine.

71 Halbrook, "Ukraine War Reintroduces U.S. Politicians to the Second Amendment."

72 "MH17 Ukraine Plane Crash: What We Know," BBC News, February 26, 2020, https://www.bbc.com/news/world-europe-28357880.

73 James Madison, "The Influence of the State and Federal Governments Compared from the New York Packet," *The Federalist Papers*: No. 46, January 29, 1788, https://avalon.law.yale.edu/18th_century/fed46.asp.

74 "Story, Joseph," in Melvin I. Urofsky, ed., *Biographical Encyclopedia of the Supreme Court* (Washington, DC: CQ Press, 2006), https://library.cqpress.com/scc/document.php?id=bioenc-427-18169-979549&v=5f4cfb51d2ae7e7d#.

75 *United States v. The Amistad*, 40 U.S. 518 (1841), https://supreme.justia.com/cases/federal/us/40/518/.

76 Judith Haydel, "Joseph Story," *The First Amendment Encyclopedia*, https://www.mtsu.edu/first-amendment/article/1361/joseph-story; "Joseph Story," *Encyclopedia Britannica*, last updated September 14, 2022, https://www.britannica.com/biography/Joseph-Story; "Joseph Story: Manuscripts, Correspondence, and Visual Materials," Curiosity Collections, Harvard Library, https://curiosity.lib.harvard.edu/joseph-story; Corydon Ireland, "Evidence of Greatness: HLS Showcases Life and Work of Joseph Story," *Harvard Law Today*, November 19, 2012, https://hls.harvard.edu/today/evidence-of-greatness-hls-showcases-life-and-work-of-joseph-story/.

77 Story, *Commentaries on the Constitution*, 3:§1890.

78 1 J. Story, Commentaries on the Constitution of the United States § 208 (1st ed. 1833).

79 Jonathan Elliot, ed., *The Debates in the Several State Conventions on the Adoption of the Federal Constitution* (1836), 3: 425.

80 *District of Columbia v. Heller*.

81 Story, *Commentaries on the Constitution*, 3:§1890, quoted in *McDonald v. City of Chicago*, 561 U.S. 742 (2010), https://supreme.justia.com/cases/federal/us/561/742/.

82 Story, *Commentaries on the Constitution*, 3:§1890.

83 See, e.g., "Guns in Ukraine," GunPolicy.org, https://www.gunpolicy.org/firearms/region/cp/ukraine.

84 "Guns in Ukraine," GunPolicy.org; Firearms News Special Report, "President Zelenskyy: Open Up Ukrainian Gun Ownership!" *Firearms News*, February 23, 2022, https://www.firearmsnews.com/editorial/president-zelenskyy-ukrainian-gun-ownership/458322; "A Law Allowing Civilians to Fight the Aggressor Has Come into Force in Ukraine," Ukrainian Gun Owners Association, ZBROYA Info, March 11, 2022, https://zbroya.info/en/blog/21599_a-law-allowing-civilians-to-fight-the-aggressor-has-come-into-force-in-ukraine/.

85 Firearms News Special Report, "President Zelenskyy: Open Up Ukrainian Gun Ownership!"

86 David Martosko, "Flashback: Senator Obama Pushed Bill That Helped Destroy More Than 15,000 TONS of Ammunition, 400,000 Small Arms and 1,000 Anti-Aircraft Missiles in Ukraine," *Daily Mail* (UK), March 5, 2014, https://www.dailymail.co.uk/news/article-2573557/Flashback-Senator-Obama-pushed-destruction-15-000-TONS-ammunition-400-000-small-arms-1-000-anti-aircraft-missiles-Ukraine.html.

87 Martosko, "Flashback: Senator Obama Pushed Bill That Helped Destroy More Than 15,000 TONS of Ammunition, 400,000 Small Arms and 1,000 Anti-Aircraft Missiles in Ukraine."

88 Eli Lake, "Exclusive: Ukraine Asked U.S. for Tech to Counter Russia's Jet-Killers," The Daily Beast, July 23, 2014, https://www.thedailybeast.com/exclusive-ukraine-asked-us-for-tech-to-counter-russias-jet-killers.

89 Andrew C. McCarthy, "Obama Won't Arm Ukraine Because He Led the Disarming of Ukraine," *National Review*, July 23, 2014, https://www.nationalreview.com/corner/obama-wont-arm-ukraine-because-he-led-disarming-ukraine-andrew-c-mccarthy/.

90 *New York State Rifle & Pistol Association, Inc. v. Bruen*, 597 U.S. ___ (2022), https://supreme.justia.com/cases/federal/us/597/20-843/.

91 Dave Carlin, "Gov. Hochul Signs Law Banning Guns in Many Public Places in New York," CBS News, July 2, 2022, https://www.cbsnews.com/newyork/news/new-york-gun-law-firearms-banned-public-places/.

92 Anders Hagstrom, "NY Gov. Hochul Defiant After Supreme Court Gun Decision: 'We're Just Getting Started,'" Fox News, June 23, 2022, https://www.foxnews.com/politics/ny-gov-hochul-defiant-supreme-court-handgun-ruling-were-just-getting-started; Gabriel Hays, "Twitter Slams Gov. Hochul's Anger over SCOTUS Gun Ruling: 'Sorry the Constitution Happened to You,'" Fox News, June 23, 2022, https://www.foxnews.com/media/twitter-slams-gov-hochuls-anger-over-scotus-gun-ruling-sorry-constitution-happened.

93 Hannah Wiley, "California Enacts Sweeping Gun Control Laws, Setting up a Legal Showdown," *Los Angeles Times*, July 12, 2022, https://www.latimes.com/california/story/2022-07-12/gavin-newsom-signs-firearm-laws-supreme-court-gun-rights.

94 Emily Cochrane and Zolan Kanno-Youngs, "Biden Signs Gun Bill into Law, Ending Years of Stalemate,"

New York Times, June 25, 2022, https://www.nytimes.com/2022/06/25/us/politics/gun-control-bill-biden.html.

95   Colonel Liam Collins and Lionel Beehner, "Dispatches from the Modern War Institute: Baltic States' Militaries Buttressed by Volunteers," Association of the United States Army, March 21, 2019, https://www.ausa.org/articles/baltic-states%E2%80%99-militaries-buttressed-volunteers.

96   Halbrook, "Ukraine War Reintroduces U.S. Politicians to the Second Amendment." For the full story, see Stephen Halbrook, *Gun Control in Nazi-Occupied France: Tyranny and Resistance* (Oakland: The Independent Institute, 2018).

97   Firearms News Special Report, "President Zelenskyy: Open Up Ukrainian Gun Ownership!"

98   Azmi Haroun, "Ukraine's Parliament Passed a Law Allowing Citizens to Carry Firearms, and a Local NGO Official Said 'There's a Feeling That Ukrainians Will Fight,'" *Business Insider*, February 23, 2022, https://www.businessinsider.com/ukraine-parliament-passes-law-allowing-citizens-to-carry-firearms-2022-2.

99   Address by the President of the Russian Federation, The Kremlin, Moscow, Feb. 21, 2022. http://en.kremlin.ru/events/president/transcripts/67828

100 The Ukrainian gun bill passed on February 23, 2022, and the invasion had commenced on or about February 24, 2022. "Ukraine Expands Civilian Gun Rights to Fight Russia," *Breitbart*, https://www.

breitbart.com/politics/2022/02/23/ukraine-expands-civilian-gun-rights-to-fight-russia/

[101] Khurshudyan, O'Grady, and Morris, "'Weapons to Anyone': Across Ukraine, Militias Form as Russian Forces Near."

[102] Sravasti Dasgupta, "Ukraine Says 40 People Killed So Far in First Hours of Russian Invasion," *Independent* (UK), February 24, 2022, https://www.independent.co.uk/news/world/europe/ukraine-war-death-toll-russia-invasion-b2022214.html.

[103] Khurshudyan, O'Grady, and Morris, "'Weapons to Anyone': Across Ukraine, Militias Form as Russian Forces Near."

[104] Aamer Madhani, Associated Press, and Geoff Ziezulewicz, "'Make Molotov Cocktails!': Battles Rage in Kyiv and Other Ukraine Cities," *Navy Times*, February 25, 2022, https://www.navytimes.com/flashpoints/2022/02/25/make-molotov-cocktails-battles-rage-in-kyiv-and-other-ukraine-cities/.

[105] Campbell MacDiarmid, "The Tracksuit Resistance: Ukrainian Civilians Grab Their AK-47s and Take on Advancing Russian Army," *Telegraph* (UK), February 26, 2022, https://www.telegraph.co.uk/world-news/2022/02/26/tracksuit-resistance-ukrainian-civilians-grab-ak-47s-take-advancing/.

[106] Hollie McKay, "Ukrainians Start Arming Themselves for Possible Russian Attack," *New York Post*, February 3, 2022, https://nypost.com/2022/02/03/ukrainians-arming-themselves-for-possible-russian-attack/.

[107] See, e.g., Oleksandr Kozhukhar and Sergiy Karazy, "Zelenskiy Demands Western Nations Give Arms to

Ukraine, Asks If They're Afraid of Moscow," Reuters, March 27, 2022, https://www.reuters.com/world/europe/ukraine-leader-demands-western-nations-give-arms-asks-if-theyre-afraid-moscow-2022-03-26/.

108 See, e.g., Aamer Madhani, Robert Burns, and Darlene Superville, "Biden Announces Heavy Artillery, Other Weapons for Ukraine," Associated Press, April 21, 2022, https://apnews.com/article/russia-ukraine-war-biden-announces-new-military-aid-e78a7db76215a84f86586b-b56122cd04; Amanda Macias, "Biden to Send Another $1 Billion in Military Aid to Ukraine," CNBC, June 15 2022, https://www.cnbc.com/2022/06/15/biden-to-send-another-1-billion-in-military-aid-to-ukraine-.html.

109 "Statement by President Joe Biden on Additional Security Assistance to Ukraine," White House, June 1, 2022, https://www.whitehouse.gov/briefing-room/statements-releases/2022/06/01/statement-by-president-joe-biden-on-additional-security-assistance-to-ukraine-2/.

110 Public Safety and Recreational Firearms Use Protection Act, Pub. L. 103–322, 108 Stat. 1796 (2004).

111 Bipartisan Safer Communities Act, Pub. L. 117–159, 136 Stat. 131 (2022).

112 Occupy Democrats, Twitter, February 24, 2022, https://twitter.com/occupydemocrats/status/1496946340521119747?lang=en.

113 Occupy Democrats, Twitter, July 11, 2022, https://twitter.com/OccupyDemocrats/status/1546530385068052480.

114 *Staples v. United States*, 511 U.S. 600 (1994), https://supreme.justia.com/cases/federal/us/511/600/.

115 Brooke Singman, "Vance Demands Biden Admin Turn Over 'Full Crosscutting' Report on Security Assistance Provided to Ukraine," Fox News, January 10, 2023, https://www.foxnews.com/politics/vance-demands-biden-admin-full-crosscutting-report-security-assistance-ukraine.

116 Portfolio Armor, "How Arming Ukraine Has Made America Weaker," ZeroHedge, January 13, 2023, https://www.zerohedge.com/news/2023-01-13/how-arming-ukraine-has-made-america-weaker.

117 Mark F. Cancian, "Will the United States Run Out of Javelins Before Russia Runs Out of Tanks?", Center for Strategic & International Studies, April 12, 2022, https://www.csis.org/analysis/will-united-states-run-out-javelins-russia-runs-out-tanks.

118 Id.

119 Id.

120 Peter Champelli, Juanje Gómez, and Daniel Nasaw, From Javelins to Tanks: What $30 Billion in U.S. Military Aid to Ukraine Looks Like, Wall Street Journal, March 2, 2023. https://www.wsj.com/articles/how-u-s-weapons-play-a-growing-role-in-the-ukraine-war-8ee548ef.

121 U.S. Department of State, Fact Sheet: U.S. Security Cooperation with Ukraine, March 3, 2023. https://www.state.gov/u-s-security-cooperation-with-ukraine/.

122 See, e.g., Hanna Duggal, How much have NATO members spent on Ukraine? Al Jazeera, February 15, 2023. https://www.aljazeera.com/news/2023/2/15/infographic-how-much-have-nato-members-spent-on-ukraine.

123 Jonathan Masters and Will Merrow, How Much Aid Has the U.S. Sent Ukraine? Here are Six Charts, Council on Foreign Relations, February 22, 2023, https://www.cfr.org/article/how-much-aid-has-us-sent-ukraine-here-are-six-charts.

124 Mackubin Owens, "Ukraine Highlights Lessons for the U.S. Defense Industrial Base," American Greatness, December 21, 2022, https://amgreatness.com/2022/12/21/ukraine-highlights-lessons-for-the-u-s-defense-industrial-base/.

125 Ukraine Law No. 2114-IX, March 3, 2022, translation available at https://cis-legislation.com/document.fwx?rgn=138407.

126 Ukraine Law No. 2114-IX.

127 See English excerpt, with link to full translation, at David Codrea, "EXCLUSIVE: Ukrainian Territorial Defense Ordered to Turn in Arms 'for Storage' Purposes," Firearms News, April 25, 2022, https://www.firearmsnews.com/editorial/ukrainian-territorial-defense-turn-in-arms/460063.; see here for full speech in Ukrainian: https://texty.org.ua/fragments/106440/dobrovolci-teroborony-u-zvilnenyh-rehionah-mayut-zdaty-zbroyu-do-misc-zberihannya-komanduvach-syl-tro-zsu. Note: Part of the quote I am using here is directly quoted by David Codrea. While a portion of the quote I am using here

was not quoted in the article, the link to the full speech and translation can be found in the Codrea article.

128 Scott McDonald, "Some Ukrainians Issued Weapons at Start of War Now Asked to Return Them," Newsweek, March 7, 2023, https://www.newsweek.com/some-ukrainians-issued-weapons-start-war-now-asked-return-them-1785912.

129 McDonald, "Some Ukrainians Issued Weapons at Start of War Now Asked to Return Them." Newsweek, March 7, 2023, https://www.newsweek.com/some-ukrainians-issued-weapons-start-war-now-asked-return-them-1785912.

130 See Constantini, "Analysis: What Ukraine's Embrace of Gun Rights as Russia Attacks Could Mean for Europe."

131 David B. Kopel, "Guns Kill People, and Tyrants with Gun Monopolies Kill the Most," *Gonzaga Journal of International Law*, no. 25 (November 6, 2022): 2021, University of Denver Legal Studies Research Paper, available at SSRN, https://ssrn.com/abstract=3942071.

132 Firearm Owners Protection Act, 18 USC 926, https://www.law.cornell.edu/uscode/text/18/926. See also Corinne Jones, "Background Checks on Gun Sales: How Do They Work?" CNN, April 10, 2013, https://www.cnn.com/2013/04/10/politics/background-checks-explainer/index.html/.

133 See Stephen P. Halbrook, *Gun Control in the Third Reich: Disarming the Jews and "Enemies of the State"* (Oakland: Independent Institute, 2013).

134 Halbrook, "Ukraine War Reintroduces U.S. Politicians to the Second Amendment."

135 "Read: U.S. Letter to the U.N. Alleging Russia Is Planning Human Rights Abuses in Ukraine," *Washington Post*, February 20, 2022, https://www.washingtonpost.com/context/read-u-s-letter-to-the-u-n-alleging-russia-is-planning-human-rights-abuses-in-ukraine/93a8d6a1-5b44-4ae8-89e5-cd5d328dd150/?itid=lk_inline_manual_4.

136 Pavlo Bakhura, "No Safe Way Out of Izyum: 'I Can't Imagine How It Will End,'" *The Guardian* (UK), April 4, 2022, https://www.theguardian.com/world/2022/apr/04/izyum-ukraine-shelling-russian-soldiers.

137 "Verkhovna Rada Passes Bill on Civilian Firearms at First Reading," Ukrainian National News Agency, February 23, 2022, https://www.ukrinform.net/rubric-defense/3410346-verkhovna-rada-passes-bill-on-civilian-firearms-at-first-reading.html.

138 "UPDATED: Mass Public Shootings Keep Occurring in Gun-Free Zones: 94% of Attacks Since 1950," Crime Prevention Research Center, updated July 6, 2019, https://crimeresearch.org/2018/06/more-misleading-information-from-bloombergs-everytown-for-gun-safety-on-guns-analysis-of-recent-mass-shootings/.

139 Carlin, "Gov. Hochul Signs Law Banning Guns in Many Public Places in New York."

140 "Verkhovna Rada Passes Bill on Civilian Firearms at First Reading."
141 Lederman and Flanagan, "Ukraine's Soldiers Have Rockets and Drones, but Are Running Low in Boots and T-Shirts."
142 Gettleman, "In Ukraine's South, Fierce Fighting and Deadly Costs."
143 Constantini, "Analysis: What Ukraine's Embrace of Gun Rights as Russia Attacks Could Mean for Europe."
144 Bubello and de Guzman, "'We Are Fighting for Survival': The Ukrainian Citizens Volunteering to Defend Their Country from Russian Troops."
145 Boot, "To Deter a Russian Attack, Ukraine Needs to Prepare for Guerrilla Warfare."
146 Bubello and de Guzman, "'We Are Fighting for Survival': The Ukrainian Citizens Volunteering to Defend Their Country from Russian Troops"; Cookman, "Ukraine's Civilian Militia Trains to Protect Kiev from Russia."
147 Cookman, "Ukraine's Civilian Militia Trains to Protect Kiev from Russia."
148 Lederman and Flanagan, "Ukraine's Soldiers Have Rockets and Drones, but Are Running Low in Boots and T-Shirts."
149 Robert Zaretsky, "The International Brigade 2.0: The Foreign Volunteers in Ukraine Follow Those Who Fought Fascism in the Spanish Civil War," *Foreign Policy*, March 20, 2022, https://foreignpolicy.com/2022/03/20/ukraine-war-foreign-volunteers-spanish-civil-war/.

150 "Russia Invaded Ukraine," Fight for Ukraine, International Legion of Defence of Ukraine, https://fightforua.org/.

151 "Every Third Ukrainian Ready to Put Up Armed Resistance to Russians," Ukrainian National News Agency, December 17, 2021, https://www.ukrinform.net/rubric-society/3371045-every-third-ukrainian-ready-to-put-up-armed-resistance-to-russians.html.

152 Andrew Wilson, "Resilient Ukraine," Royal United Services Institute, July 7, 2022, https://rusi.org/explore-our-research/publications/commentary/resilient-ukraine.

153 Harding, "Business Brisk at Kyiv Gun Shops as Ukrainians Rush to Buy Arms."

154 Halbrook, "Ukraine War Reintroduces U.S. Politicians to the Second Amendment."

155 McKay, "Ukrainians Start Arming Themselves for Possible Russian Attack."

156 McKay, "Ukrainians Start Arming Themselves for Possible Russian Attack."

157 Yaron Steinbuch, "Ukrainian Mom Buys Powerful Hunting Rifle, Vows to 'Fight for Kiev,'" *New York Post*, February 3, 2022, https://nypost.com/2022/01/26/ukrainian-mom-mariana-zhaglo-buys-rifle-will-fight-for-kiev/.

158 Antonia Cundy, "'Women Need to Be Ready': The Ukrainian City Where Mums and Daughters Are Learning to Shoot," *The Guardian* (UK), April 25, 2022, https://www.theguardian.com/global-development/2022/

apr/25/women-need-to-be-ready-the-ukrainian-city-where-mums-and-daughters-are-learning-to-shoot.

[159] Anna Brovko, "'You Need to Know How to Shoot': Lviv Students Are Taught the ABCs of Self-Defense," Radio Free Europe/Radio Liberty, August 1, 2022, https://www.rferl.org/a/ukraine-children-war-russia-security-/31969169.html.

[160] Hannah McCarthy, "Gun School: Ukraine Rolls Out Weapons Training for Civilians," *Irish Examiner*, March 14, 2022, https://www.irishexaminer.com/news/spotlight/arid-40828439.html.

[161] Anne Applebaum, "The Other Ukrainian Army," *The Atlantic*, August 10, 2022, https://www.theatlantic.com/ideas/archive/2022/08/ukraine-volunteer-army-russia-odesa/671088/.

[162] Lederman and Flanagan, "Ukraine's Soldiers Have Rockets and Drones, but Are Running Low in Boots and T-Shirts."

[163] Carol Schaeffer, "Why So Many Ukrainians Are Returning Home," *The Nation*, April 28, 2022, https://www.thenation.com/article/world/ukraine-return-europe/; Belle de Jong, "Half a Million Refugees Return to Ukraine to Help War Effort," *Brussels Times* (Belgium), March 29, 2022, https://www.brusselstimes.com/213482/ukrainian-spirit-half-a-million-refugees-returned-to-their-country.

[164] Mogelson, "How Ukrainians Saved Their Capital."

[165] Constantini, "Analysis: What Ukraine's Embrace of Gun Rights as Russia Attacks Could Mean for Europe."

[166] Kornick, "Biden Blasted for Mocking 'Brave' Second Amendment Defenders: 'You Need an F-15' to Fight America, Not a Gun."

167 "Remarks by President Biden After Marine One Arrival," White House, May 30, 2022, https://www.whitehouse.gov/briefing-room/speeches-remarks/2022/05/30/remarks-by-president-biden-after-marine-one-arrival-10/.

168 Sinéad Baker, "Biden Mocked Gun-Rights Advocates Who Say They Need Assault Weapons to Fight the Government: 'You Need F-15s and Maybe Some Nuclear Weapons,'" *Business Insider*, June 24, 2021, https://www.businessinsider.com/biden-mocks-gun-right-advocates-who-say-assault-weapons-needed-fight-government-2021-6.

169 David Harsanyi, "Joe Biden's Incoherent Second Amendment Rant," *National Review*, February 10, 2020, https://www.nationalreview.com/2020/02/joe-biden-gun-rights-doesnt-understand-second-amendment/.

170 Amy Swearer, "The 5 Most Unserious Things Biden Said in His Gun Control Speech," Daily Signal, September 9, 2022, https://www.dailysignal.com/2022/09/09/the-5-most-unserious-things-biden-said-in-his-gun-control-speech/.

171 Poppy Koronka, "The 20 Most Powerful Military Forces in the World," *Newsweek*, August 24, 2021, https://www.newsweek.com/most-powerful-military-forces-world-america-china-russia-1621130; "2023 Military Strength Ranking," Global Firepower, undated, https://www.globalfirepower.com/countries-listing.php.

172 David Brown, Jake Horton, and Tural Ahmedzade, "Ukraine Weapons: What Military Equipment Is the

World Giving?" BBC News, September 9, 2022, https://www.bbc.com/news/world-europe-62002218.

173 Sanford Levinson, "The NRA Didn't Help," Letter to the Editor, *New York Review of Books*, August 18, 2016, https://www.nybooks.com/articles/2016/08/18/the-nra-didnt-help/.

174 Sanford Levinson, "The Embarrassing Second Amendment," *Yale Law Journal* 99, no. 3 (December 1989), https://www.jstor.org/stable/796759.

175 Angela Dewan, "Ukraine and Russia's Militaries Are David and Goliath. Here's How They Compare," CNN, February 25, 2022, https://www.cnn.com/2022/02/25/europe/russia-ukraine-military-comparison-intl/index.html.

176 Maria Varenikova and Andrew E. Kramer, "How Ukraine's Outgunned Air Force Is Fighting Back Against Russian Jets," *New York Times*, March 22, 2022, https://www.nytimes.com/2022/03/22/world/europe/ukraine-air-force-russia.html.

177 Alex Horton, Claire Parker, and Dalton Bennett, "On the Battlefield, Ukraine Uses Soviet-Era Weapons Against Russia," *Washington Post*, April 29, 2022, https://www.washingtonpost.com/world/2022/04/29/urkaine-russian-soviet-weapons/.

178 Joseph Trevithick, "Needy Ukrainian Reserve Units Could Be Armed with Pre–World War II DP-27 Machine Guns," *The Drive/The War Zone*, March 10, 2022, https://www.thedrive.com/the-war-zone/44034/pre-world-war-ii-dp-27-machine-guns-could-go-to-needy-ukrainian-reserve-units.

179 Dewan, "Ukraine and Russia's Militaries Are David and Goliath. Here's How They Compare."
180 Bureau of Political-Military Affairs, "Fact Sheet: U.S. Security Cooperation with Ukraine"; "Fact Sheet on U.S. Security Assistance for Ukraine."
181 Caroline Elliott, "American Gun Manufacturer Sending Thousands of AR-15s to Ukraine," Fox Business, https://www.foxbusiness.com/small-business/american-gun-manufacturer-ar-15s-ukraine; Eric Sof, "UAR-15: A New Ukrainian Clone of the AR-15 Rifle Intended to Replace Kalashnikov," *Spec Ops*, May 21, 2022, https://special-ops.org/uar-15-zbroyar-z-15-rifle/.
182 Cohen, "Ukraine Receives Weapons Support from Around the World."
183 Matthew Moss, "Small Arms of the War in Ukraine," The Firearm Blog, March 23, 2022, https://www.thefirearmblog.com/blog/2022/03/23/small-arms-of-the-war-in-ukraine/.
184 Mark Chesnut, "NSSF Helping Streamline Manufacturer Efforts to Arm Ukraine," *Firearms News*, March 17, 2022, https://www.firearmsnews.com/editorial/nssf-streamline-efforts-arm-ukraine/458992.
185 Moss, "Small Arms of the War in Ukraine." See also "List of Russo-Ukrainian Conflict Military Equipment," Wikipedia, https://en.wikipedia.org/wiki/List_of_Russo-Ukrainian_conflict_military_equipment#Small_arms_2.

186 Lederman and Flanagan, "Ukraine's Soldiers Have Rockets and Drones, but Are Running Low in Boots and T-Shirts."
187 Tom Batchelor and Jane Dalton, "Russian Major General Andrei Sukhovetsky Killed by Ukrainians in 'Major Demotivator' for Invading Army," *Independent* (UK), March 7, 2022, https://www.independent.co.uk/news/world/europe/andrei-sukhovetsky-russian-general-killed-b2029363.html.
188 William Booth, Robyn Dixon, and David L. Stern, "Russian Generals Are Getting Killed at an Extraordinary Rate," *Washington Post*, March 26, 2022, https://www.washingtonpost.com/world/2022/03/26/ukraine-russan-generals-dead/.
189 David Meyer, "'Snipers Have Been Picking Them Off Left and Right': Retired U.S. General Explains Why So Many Russian Generals Are Getting Killed in Ukraine," *Fortune*, March 21, 2022, https://fortune.com/2022/03/21/ukraine-snipers-russia-generals-mordvichev-mariupol-ncos-david-petraeus/.
190 Matt Murphy, "Ukraine War: Another Russian General Killed by Ukrainian Forces—Reports," BBC News, June 6, 2022, https://www.bbc.com/news/world-europe-61702862.
191 Julian E. Barnes, Helene Cooper, and Eric Schmitt, "U.S. Intelligence Is Helping Ukraine Kill Russian Generals, Officials Say," *New York Times*, May 4, 2022, https://www.nytimes.com/2022/05/04/us/politics/russia-generals-killed-ukraine.html.
192 Meyer, "'Snipers Have Been Picking Them Off Left and Right': Retired U.S. General Explains Why So Many Russian Generals Are Getting Killed in Ukraine."

193 Brendan Cole, "Putin Loses Another Top Soldier as 'The Executioner' Killed by Sniper," *Newsweek*, June 7, 2022, https://www.newsweek.com/putin-russia-ukraine-andanov-general-wagner-mercenary-1713368; Snejana Farberov, "Putin's Mercenary Dubbed 'The Executioner' Killed by Ukrainian Sniper: Reports," *New York Post*, June 7, 2022, https://nypost.com/2022/06/07/putin-mercenary-vladimir-andonov-killed-by-sniper-reports/.

194 Maxim Tucker, "War in Ukraine: We've Taken Out 300 Russian Troops, Say Zelensky's Special Forces," *The Times* (UK), June 21, 2022, https://www.thetimes.co.uk/article/war-in-ukraine-weve-taken-out-300-russian-troops-say-zelenskys-snipers-ct6zgbjgb.

195 Zenger News, "Ukrainian Special Forces Sniper Takes Out Group of Russian Soldiers," YouTube, June 30, 2022, https://www.youtube.com/watch?v=wwi-y26nC_PE; Joseph Golder, "Ukrainian Special Forces Snipers Take Out Russian Troops," Zenger News, August 4, 2022, https://www.zenger.news/2022/08/04/ukrainian-special-forces-snipers-take-out-russian-troops/.

196 See, e.g., Eric Schmitt, Helene Cooper, and Julian E. Barnes, "How Ukraine's Military Has Resisted Russia So Far," *New York Times*, March 3, 2022, https://www.nytimes.com/2022/03/03/us/politics/russia-ukraine-military.html; Julian E. Barnes, "Why the U.S. Was Wrong About Ukraine and the Afghan War," *New York Times*, March 24, 2022, https://www.nytimes.

com/2022/03/24/us/politics/intelligence-agencies-ukraine-afghanistan.html; Phillips Payson O'Brien, "How the West Got Russia's Military So, So Wrong," *The Atlantic*, March 31, 2022, https://www.theatlantic.com/ideas/archive/2022/03/russia-ukraine-invasion-military-predictions/629418/; Sébastien Roblin, "The Secret to the Ukrainian Military's Success," NBC News, March 31, 2022, https://www.nbcnews.com/think/opinion/russian-ukraine-war-ukrainian-army-winning-rcna22415; Nomaan Merchant and Matthew Lee, "U.S. Intelligence Agencies Review What They Got Wrong on Russia's Invasion of Ukraine," Associated Press, PBS, June 4, 2022, https://www.pbs.org/newshour/nation/u-s-intelligence-agencies-review-what-they-got-wrong-on-russias-invasion-of-ukraine; Franz-Stefan Gady, "Predicting Military Performance Can't Be Perfect. But It Can Be Better," *World Politics Review*, July 18, 2022, https://www.worldpoliticsreview.com/how-analysts-got-military-russia-invasion-of-ukraine-wrong/.

[197] Daniel Treisman, "6 Lessons the West Has Learned in the 6 Months After Russia's Invasion of Ukraine," CNN, August 23, 2022, https://www.cnn.com/2022/08/22/opinions/putin-russia-invasion-ukraine-treisman/index.html.

[198] Jacqui Heinrich and Adam Sabes, "Gen. Milley Says Kyiv Could Fall Within 72 hours If Russia Decides to Invade Ukraine: Sources."

[199] Robert Burns, "Russia's Failure to Take Down Kyiv Was a Defeat for the Ages," Associated Press, April 7, 2022,

https://apnews.com/article/russia-ukraine-war-battle-for-kyiv-dc559574ce9f6683668fa221af2d5340.

200 James Marson, "Putin Thought Ukraine Would Fall Quickly. An Airport Battle Proved Him Wrong," *Wall Street Journal*, March 3, 2022, https://www.wsj.com/articles/putin-thought-ukraine-would-fall-quickly-an-airport-battle-proved-him-wrong-11646343121. See also Burns, "Russia's Failure to Take Down Kyiv Was a Defeat for the Ages"; Stijn Mitzer and Joost Oliemans, "Destination Disaster: Russia's Failure at Hostomel Airport," Oryx, April 13, 2022, https://www.oryxspioenkop.com/2022/04/destination-disaster-russias-failure-at.html.

201 Amy Mackinnon, "The Tide Has Already Turned in Ukraine's Favor," *Foreign Policy*, September 14, 2022, https://foreignpolicy.com/2022/09/14/jack-watling-interview-ukraine-russia-war/; Tom Soufi Burridge, Patrick Reevell, Dragana Jovanovic, and Oleksiy Pshemyskiy, "Ukraine Recaptures Swath of Land in 'Breakthrough' Offensive," ABC News, September 10, 2022, https://abcnews.go.com/International/ukraine-recaptures-swath-land-breakthrough-offensive/story?id=89644247.

202 Simon Shuster, "2022 Person of the Year, Volodymyr Zelensky," *Time*, December 26, 2022/January 9, 2023, https://time.com/person-of-the-year-2022-volodymyr-zelensky/.

203 Sébastien Roblin, "Why U.S. Military Aid Is Working in Ukraine," NBC News, May 15, 2022, https://www.nbcnews.com/think/opinion/ukraine-military-war-russia-us-aid-weapons-rcna28830.

204 Roblin, "Why U.S. Military Aid Is Working in Ukraine."
205 Max Boot, *Invisible Armies: An Epic History of Invisible Warfare from Ancient Times to the Present* (New York: Liveright, 2013), xxvi.
206 Bob Zeller, "The Tipping Point: From French Arms to French Fleets, How France Changed the Tides of the American Revolution," American Battlefield Trust, June 25, 2018, https://www.battlefields.org/learn/articles/how-france-helped-win-american-revolution.
207 Christopher Klein, "7 Ways the Battle of Antietam Changed America," History Stories, History.com, August 31, 2018, https://www.history.com/news/7-ways-the-battle-of-antietam-changed-america; Howard Jones, *Blue and Gray Diplomacy: A History of Union and Confederate Foreign Relations* (Chapel Hill: University of North Carolina Press, 2010), 318–19.
208 Mogelson, "How Ukrainians Saved Their Capital."
209 "Ukrainian Civilians Continue to Fight for Their Country," video, NBC Nightly News, February 26, 2022, https://www.nbcnews.com/nightly-news/video/ukrainian-civilians-continue-to-fight-for-their-country-134134341791.
210 Kramer, "'Everybody in Our Country Needs to Defend.'"
211 Marson, "The Ragtag Army That Won the Battle of Kyiv and Saved Ukraine."
212 Marson, "The Ragtag Army That Won the Battle of Kyiv and Saved Ukraine."

213 Marson, "The Ragtag Army That Won the Battle of Kyiv and Saved Ukraine."
214 Olga Tokariuk, "How Ukrainian Citizens Are Mobilizing to Provide Aid and Supplies in the Fight Against Russia," *Time*, March 11, 2022, https://time.com/6156886/ukrainian-citizens-mobilizing-against-russia/.
215 Christina Olha Jarymowycz, "POV: Ukrainian Civilians Are Flipping the Script of Warfare," *BU Today*, March 15, 2022, https://www.bu.edu/articles/2022/pov-ukrainian-civilians-are-flipping-the-script-of-warfare/.
216 Marson, "The Ragtag Army That Won the Battle of Kyiv and Saved Ukraine."
217 Marson, "The Ragtag Army That Won the Battle of Kyiv and Saved Ukraine."
218 Kramer, "'Everybody in Our Country Needs to Defend.'"
219 "'Hand-to-Hand Combat': Street Battles Rage on Kyiv's Edge," France 24, Agence France Presse, March 7, 2022, https://www.france24.com/en/live-news/20220307-hand-to-hand-combat-street-battles-rage-on-kyiv-s-edge; Thomson Reuters, "'Fierce Street Fights' Continue in Ukraine's East Amid Concerns Over Grain in Occupied Regions," CBC News, June 11, 2022, https://www.cbc.ca/news/world/ukraine-russia-war-invasion-day-108-1.6485776; "Street-to-Street Fighting Reported in Ukraine's Sievierodonetsk," VOA News, June 6, 2022, https://www.voanews.com/a/street-to-street-fighting-reported-in-ukraine-s-sievierodonetsk-/6605260.

html; Kristin Ljungkvist, "New Horizon in Urban Warfare in Ukraine?" *Scandinavian Journal of Military Studies* 5, no. 1 (2022), https://sjms.nu/articles/10.31374/sjms.165/; Todd South, "Urban Combat Veterans Share Lessons for Ukraine Fight," *Military Times*, March 11, 2022, https://www.militarytimes.com/flashpoints/ukraine/2022/03/11/urban-combat-veterans-share-lessons-for-ukraine-fight/.

220 John Spencer, Lionel Beehner, and Liam Collins, "Why Russia Likely Won't Win the Fight in Ukraine's Cities," *Los Angeles Times*, April 18, 2022, https://www.latimes.com/opinion/story/2022-04-18/ukraine-russia-mariupol-urban-warfare.

221 Benjamin Phocas and Jayson Geroux, "The School of Street Fighting: Tactical Urban Lessons from Ukraine," Modern War Institute at West Point, July 13, 2022, https://mwi.usma.edu/the-school-of-street-fighting-tactical-urban-lessons-from-ukraine/.

222 Aaron Steckelberg, Adam Taylor, Ruby Mellen, Alex Horton, and Dylan Moriarty, "Why Russia Gave Up on Urban War in Kyiv and Turned to Big Battles in the East," *Washington Post*, April 15, 2022, https://www.washingtonpost.com/world/interactive/2022/kyiv-urban-warfare-russia-siege-donbas/.

223 South, "Urban Combat Veterans Share Lessons for Ukraine Fight."

224 Spencer, Beehner, and Collins, "Why Russia Likely Won't Win the Fight in Ukraine's Cities."

225 Lee Hockstader, "Chechens Dig In, Block Russian Tanks," *Washington Post*, December 16, 1994, https://www.washingtonpost.com/archive/politics/1994/12/16/chechens-dig-in-block-russian-tanks/9f966050-ea0d-44eb-8947-edad442b895d/; Major Raymond C. Finch III, "Why the Russian Military Failed in Chechnya," FMSO Special Study No 98-16, August 1998, https://apps.dtic.mil/sti/pdfs/ADA435005.pdf.

226 Antony Beevor, *Stalingrad: The Fateful Siege: 1942–1943* (New York: Penguin, 1999), 149.

227 Lloyd Clark, *The Battle of the Tanks: Kursk, 1943* (New York: Grove Atlantic, 2011).

228 Beevor, *Stalingrad*, 203–4.

229 Nicholas Slayton, "'Mad Max'–Style Technicals Have Become a Staple of Ukraine's Fight Against Russia," Task and Purpose, June 12, 2022, https://taskandpurpose.com/news/why-mad-max-style-technicals-have-become-a-staple-of-ukraines-fight-against-russia/.

230 Steve Hendrix, Serhii Korolchuk, and Robyn Dixon, "Amid Ukraine's Startling Gains, Liberated Villages Describe Russian Troops Dropping Rifles and Fleeing," *Washington Post*, September 11, 2022, https://www.washingtonpost.com/world/2022/09/11/kharkiv-liberated-retreat-izyum-russia/.

231 "Attack On Europe: Documenting Russian Equipment Losses During the 2022 Russian Invasion of Ukraine," Oryx, retrieved September 16, 2022, https://www.oryxspioenkop.com/2022/02/attack-on-europe-documenting-equipment.html.

232. Greg Myre, "How Ukraine Broke the Stalemate with Russia," *All Things Considered*, September 12, 2022, https://www.npr.org/2022/09/12/1122481686/how-ukraine-broke-the-stalemate-with-russia.

233. Ellie Kaufman, "First on CNN: Us Left Behind $7 Billion of Military Equipment in Afghanistan After 2021 Withdrawal, Pentagon Report Says," CNN, April 28, 2022, https://www.cnn.com/2022/04/27/politics/afghan-weapons-left-behind/index.html; Jonny Hallam and Mick Krever, "Taliban Show Off Captured Weapons at Kandahar Victory Parade," CNN, September 2, 2021, https://www.cnn.com/2021/09/01/asia/taliban-kandahar-captured-weapons-intl/index.html; Idrees Ali, Patricia Zengerle, and Jonathan Landay, "Planes, Guns, Night-Vision Goggles: The Taliban's New U.S.-Made War Chest," Reuters, August 19, 2021, https://www.reuters.com/business/aerospace-defense/planes-guns-night-vision-goggles-talibans-new-us-made-war-chest-2021-08-19/.

234. Yaroslav Trofimov, "Ukraine's New Offensive Is Fueled by Captured Russian Weapons," *Wall Street Journal*, October 5, 2022, https://www.wsj.com/articles/ukraines-new-offensive-is-fueled-by-captured-russian-weapons-11664965264.

235. Trofimov, "Ukraine's New Offensive Is Fueled by Captured Russian Weapons."

236. "Ukraine Defies Russia with Attacks on Crimea, a 'Holy Land' to Putin," *New York Times*, August 16, 2022, https://www.nytimes.com/live/2022/08/16/world/ukraine-russia-news-war.

237 Henry A. Kissinger, "The Viet Nam Negotiations," *Foreign Affairs* 47, no. 2 (January 1969), https://www.jstor.org/stable/20039369.

238 Paul Kirby, "Has Putin's War Failed and What Does Russia Want from Ukraine," BBC News, February 24, 2023, https://www.bbc.com/news/world-europe-56720589.

239 Kissinger, "The Viet Nam Negotiations."

240 Ron Avery, "The Story of Valley Forge," USHistory.org, https://www.ushistory.org/valleyforge/history/vstory.html.

241 Martha K. Robinson, "British Occupation of Philadelphia," *Philadelphia Encyclopedia*, https://philadelphiaencyclopedia.org/essays/british-occupation-of-philadelphia/; "This Day in History: June 18: British Abandon Philadelphia," History.com, https://www.history.com/this-day-in-history/british-abandon-philadelphia.

242 "What Is Ukraine?" Ukrainian History and Education Center, https://www.ukrhec.org/what-is-ukraine.

243 Seth G. Jones, "Russia's Ill-Fated Invasion of Ukraine: Lessons in Modern Warfare," Center for Strategic and International Studies, June 1, 2022, https://www.csis.org/analysis/russias-ill-fated-invasion-ukraine-lessons-modern-warfare.

244 Trofimov, "Ukraine's New Offensive Is Fueled by Captured Russian Weapons."

245 Kissinger, "The Viet Nam Negotiations."

246 Anika Binnendijk and Marta Kepe, "Civilian-Based Resistance in the Baltic States: Historical Precedents and

247 Binnendijk and Kepe, "Civilian-Based Resistance in the Baltic States."

248 Igor Kossov, "A glance into Kherson's underground resistance during Russian occupation," *Kyiv Independent*, December 28, 2022, https://kyivindependent.com/national/a-glance-in-to-khersons-underground-resistance-during-russian-occupation.

249 Kossov, "A glance into Kherson's underground resistance during Russian occupation."

250 Spencer, Beehner, and Collins, "Why Russia Likely Won't Win the Fight in Ukraine's Cities."

251 Spencer, Beehner, and Collins, "Why Russia Likely Won't Win the Fight in Ukraine's Cities."

252 Scott Beauchamp, "America's Misplaced Faith in Bombing Campaigns," *The Atlantic*, January 30, 2016, https://www.theatlantic.com/politics/archive/2016/01/bombs-away/433845/.

253 Jay Reynolds, "US Strategic Bombing in the Vietnam War: Success or Failure?" The Collector, October 8, 2021, https://www.thecollector.com/us-strategic-bombing-in-the-vietnam-war-success-or-failure/. See also Robert Farley, "How US Aerial Bombing During the Vietnam War Backfired," *The Diplomat*, August 11, 2016, https://thediplomat.com/2016/08/how-us-aerial-bombing-during-the-vietnam-war-backfired/.

254 Boot, *Invisible Armies*, xx.

255 Boot, "To Deter a Russian Attack, Ukraine Needs to Prepare for Guerrilla Warfare."

256 Bernd Greiner, *War Without Fronts: The USA in Vietnam* (London: Bodley Head, 2009), 144.

257 John T. Correll, "What Happened to Shock and Awe?" *Air Force Magazine*, November 1, 2003, https://www.airforcemag.com/article/1103shock/.

258 Alex de Waal, "Sudan: Patterns of Violence and Imperfect Endings," in Bridget Conley-Zilkic, ed., *How Mass Atrocities End: Studies from Guatemala, Burundi, Indonesia, Sudan, Bosnia-Herzegovina, and Iraq* (Cambridge: Cambridge University Press, 2016), quoted in David B. Kopel, "Guns Kill People, and Tyrants with Gun Monopolies Kill the Most," *Gonzaga Journal of International Law* 25, no. 1 (Fall 2021), https://gjil.scholasticahq.com/article/40361-guns-kill-people-and-tyrants-with-gun-monopolies-kill-the-most.

259 Boot, "To Deter a Russian Attack, Ukraine Needs to Prepare for Guerrilla Warfare."

260 Todd S. Sechser, "Putin Is Discovering That Overwhelming Military Power Can Be a Curse," *Washington Post*, March 29, 2022, https://www.washingtonpost.com/politics/2022/03/29/putin-is-discovering-that-having-overwhelming-military-power-can-be-curse/.

261 Sechser, "Putin Is Discovering That Overwhelming Military Power Can Be a Curse."

262 Simon Worrall, "Inside the Daring Mission That Thwarted a Nazi Atomic Bomb," *National Geographic*, June 5, 2016, https://www.nationalgeographic.com/history/article/winter-fortress-neal-bascomb-heroes-of-telemark-nazi-atomic-bomb-heavy-water.

263 Worrall, "Inside the Daring Mission That Thwarted a Nazi Atomic Bomb."

264 "Battle of the Alamo," History.com, January 12, 2021, https://www.history.com/topics/mexico/alamo; "Remember the Alamo," The Alamo, https://www.thealamo.org/remember.

265 Boot, *Invisible Armies*, xv.

266 The Editors of the Encyclopedia Britannica, "Peninsular War," *Encyclopedia Britannica*, https://www.britannica.com/event/Peninsular-War.

267 Kat Eschner, "The Midnight Ride of Paul Revere and Some Other Guys," *Smithsonian Magazine*, April 18, 2017, https://www.smithsonianmag.com/smart-news/midnight-ride-paul-revere-and-some-other-guys-180962866/.

268 "Battles of Lexington and Concord," History.com, January 14, 2020, https://www.history.com/topics/american-revolution/battles-of-lexington-and-concord; "Battles of Lexington and Concord," National Army Museum, https://www.nam.ac.uk/explore/battle-lexington-and-concord.

269 "Battles of Lexington and Concord," History.com; "Battles of Lexington and Concord," National Army Museum.

270 Stephen P. Halbrook, The Right to Bear Arms: A Constitutional Right of the People or a Privilege of the Ruling Class? 142 (2021):

271 Boot, *Invisible Armies*, 69.

272 Boot, *Invisible Armies*, 69–73.

273 David Fleet, "'We Are Fighting for Our Country,'" The Citizen, March 3, 2022, https://thecitizenonline.com/we-are-fighting-for-our-country/.

274 Donald Sommerville and Kate Lohnes, "Battle of Thermopylae," *EncyclopediaBritannica*, https://www.britannica.com/event/Battle-of-Thermopylae-Greek-history-480-BC.

275 Kopel, "Guns Kill People, and Tyrants with Gun Monopolies Kill the Most."

276 Kopel, "Guns Kill People, and Tyrants with Gun Monopolies Kill the Most."

277 *District of Columbia v. Heller*, 554 U.S. 570 (2008), https://supreme.justia.com/cases/federal/us/554/570/.

278 Wood, "How the Finns Deter Russian Invasion."

279 Militia Act of 1792, https://www.mountvernon.org/education/primary-sources-2/article/militia-act-of-1792.

280 "Minimum Age to Purchase and Possess," Giffords Law Center to Prevent Gun Violence, https://giffords.org/lawcenter/gun-laws/policy-areas/who-can-have-a-gun/minimum-age/.

281 *Military Obligation: The American Tradition*, vol. 2, part 6, *Massachusetts Enactments* (Washington, DC: Selective Service System, 1947), 159.

282. "An Act for the Regulating of the Militia," *Acts and Laws, Passed by the General Court or Assemblies of His Majesty's Province of New-Hampshire in New-England* (1716), 91–92, linked under "Primary Historical Sources," ClaytonCramer.com, http://www.claytoncramer.com/primary/primary.html.

283. "An Act for Establishing a Militia Within This Government," *Laws of the Government of New-Castle, Kent, and Sussex upon Delaware* (1742), linked under "Primary Historical Sources," ClaytonCramer.com.

284. "An Act for Amending the Several Laws for Regulating and Disciplining the Militia, and Guarding Against Invasions and Insurrections," in *Military Obligation: The American Tradition*, vol. 2, part 14, *Virginia Enactments*, 422–25.

285. "A Brief History of the NRA," National Rifle Association, https://home.nra.org/about-the-nra/.

286. "About," Civilian Marksmanship Program, https://thecmp.org/about/.

287. "About," Civilian Marksmanship Program; "National Matches," Civilian Marksmanship Program, https://thecmp.org/cmp-national-matches/.

288. Wood, "How the Finns Deter Russian Invasion."

289. Mogelson, "How Ukrainians Saved Their Capital."

290. Wood, "How the Finns Deter Russian Invasion."

291. Michael Hunt, "As Finland Considers NATO Membership, Citizens Mobilize for an Invasion by Russia," *Los Angeles Times*, April 24, 2022, https://www.latimes.com/world-nation/

story/2022-04-24/as-finland-considers-nato-membership-citizens-mobilize-for-an-invasion-by-russia.

292 Hunt, "As Finland Considers NATO Membership, Citizens Mobilize for an Invasion by Russia."

293 Stephanie Yang, "Fears of a Chinese Invasion Have Taiwanese Civilians Taking Up Target Practice," *Los Angeles Times*, May 26, 2022, https://www.latimes.com/world-nation/story/2022-05-26/taiwan-civilians-china-invasion-defense-training-bb-airsoft-guns.

294 Yang, "Fears of a Chinese Invasion Have Taiwanese Civilians Taking Up Target Practice."

295 Wood, "How the Finns Deter Russian Invasion."

296 See, e.g., Julian E. Barnes, "Russia's Invasion of Ukraine Looks Like a 'Failure,' C.I.A. Director Says," *New York Times*, September 8, 2022, https://www.nytimes.com/2022/09/08/world/europe/putin-russia-ukraine-cia.html; Nomaan Merchant and Eric Tucker, "Russia Underestimated Ukraine's Resistance, US Officials Say," Associated Press, March 8, 2022, https://apnews.com/article/russia-ukraine-putin-biden-europe-avril-haines-5c9707de86165915e7ce9d10d18464f3; David J. Kramer, "Never Underestimate Ukrainians," The Catalyst, Spring 2022, https://www.bushcenter.org/catalyst/ukraine/kramer-never-underestimate-ukrainians.htm; Taras Kuzio, "Putin Believed His Own Propaganda and Fatally Underestimated Ukraine," Atlantic Council, July 28, 2022, https://www.atlanticcouncil.org/blogs/ukrainealert/putin-believed-his-own-propaganda-and-fatally-underestimated-ukraine/.

297 John Heubusch, "Peace Through Strength, Across the Centuries: True Then, True Today," *National Interest*, August 19, 2016, https://nationalinterest.org/blog/the-buzz/peace-through-strength-across-the-centuries-true-then-true-17511.

298 Boot, "To Deter a Russian Attack, Ukraine Needs to Prepare for Guerrilla Warfare."

299 First Annual Message of George Washington, January 8, 1790, https://avalon.law.yale.edu/18th_century/washs05.asp.

300 Susan Ratcliffe, ed., *Oxford Essential Quotations*, 6th ed. (New York: Oxford University Press, 2018), https://www.oxfordreference.com/view/10.1093/acref/9780191866692.001.0001/q-oro-ed6-00011152#:~:text=Qui%20desiderat%20pacem%2C%20praeparet%20bellum,desires%20peace%2C%20prepare%20for%20war.

301 The Editors of the Encyclopedia Britannica, "Vegetius," *Encyclopedia Britannica*, https://www.britannica.com/biography/Vegetius.

302 The Editors of the Encyclopedia Britannica, "Vegetius."

303 Fifth Annual Message of George Washington, December 3, 1793, https://avalon.law.yale.edu/18th_century/washs05.asp.

304 Fifth Annual Message of George Washington.

305 First Annual Message of George Washington.

306 Liam Collins and John Spencer, "How Volunteers Can Help Defeat Great Powers," *Military Times*, July 5, 2022, https://www.militarytimes.com/opinion/commentary/2022/07/05/how-volunteers-can-defeat-great-powers/.

307 Collins and Spencer, "How Volunteers Can Help Defeat Great Powers."
308 Collins and Spencer, "How Volunteers Can Help Defeat Great Powers."
309 Colonel Liam Collins and Lionel Beehner, "Dispatches from the Modern War Institute: Baltic States' Militaries Buttressed by Volunteers," Association of the United States Army, March 21, 2019, https://www.ausa.org/articles/baltic-states%E2%80%99-militaries-buttressed-volunteers.
310 Collins and Beehner, "Dispatches from the Modern War Institute: Baltic States' Militaries Buttressed by Volunteers."
311 Collins and Beehner, "Dispatches from the Modern War Institute: Baltic States' Militaries Buttressed by Volunteers."
312 Collins and Beehner, "Dispatches from the Modern War Institute: Baltic States' Militaries Buttressed by Volunteers."
313 Kissinger, "The Viet Nam Negotiations."
314 Collins and Spencer, "How Volunteers Can Help Defeat Great Powers."
315 Zachary Basu, "Finland and Sweden Bring Military Might to NATO," Axios, May 18, 2022, https://www.axios.com/2022/05/19/nato-finland-sweden-military-might.
316 Wood, "How the Finns Deter Russian Invasion."
317 Darragh Roche, "What Would Happen If Russia Invaded Finland? Experts Weigh In," *Newsweek*, April 14, 2022, https://www.newsweek.com/what-would-happen-russia-invaded-finland-nato-ukraine-1697956.

318 "Neutrality," SWI SwissInfo.ch, June 23, 2022, https://www.swissinfo.ch/eng/neutrality/29289102.

319 Emma Jane Kirby, "Switzerland Guns: Living with Firearms the Swiss Way," BBC News, February 11, 2013, https://www.bbc.com/news/magazine-21379912.

320 "Soldiers Can Keep Guns at Home but Not Ammo," SWI SwissInfo.ch, September 27, 2007, https://www.swissinfo.ch/eng/soldiers-can-keep-guns-at-home-but-not-ammo/970614; David B. Kopel and Stephen D'Andrilli, "The Swiss and Their Guns," *American Rifleman*, February 1990, https://davekopel.org/2A/Foreign/swiss-and-their-guns.html.

321 James Stavridis, "Putin's New Cannon Fodder Won't Win the Ukraine War," Bloomberg, September 21, 2022, https://www.bloomberg.com/opinion/articles/2022-09-21/putin-s-desperate-military-call-up-won-t-win-the-ukraine-war.

322 Jennifer Latson, "Switzerland Takes a Side for Neutrality," *Time*, February 13, 2015, https://time.com/3695334/switzerland-neutrality-history/.

323 Tamás Orbán, "Swiss Neutrality: The Anatomy of Success," Danube Institute, April 1, 2022, https://danubeinstitute.hu/en/research/swiss-neutrality-the-anatomy-of-success.

324 Stephen P. Halbrook, *Target Switzerland: Swiss Armed Neutrality in World War II* (Cambridge, MA: Da Capo Press, 1998).

325 Halbrook, *Target Switzerland*.

326 "Zbroyar—10.5″ SBR AR-15 from Ukraine," The Firearm Blog, March 24, 2016, https://www.thefirearmblog.com/blog/2016/03/24/zbroyar-10-5-sbr-ar-15-ukraine/.

327 Quoted in David B. Kopel, Paul Gallant, and Joanne D. Eisen, "Gun Control and the Right to Arms After 9/11: The Day that Changed Everything?" in Matthew J. Morgan, ed., The Impact of 9/11 and the New Legal Landscape (New York: Palgrave Macmillan, 2009), 83.

328 Nelson Lund, "The Second Amendment, Political Liberty, and the Right to Self-Preservation," *Alabama Law Review* 39 (1987): 103, https://heinonline.org/HOL/LandingPage?handle=hein.journals/bamalr39&div=9&id=&page=.

329 David B. Kopel, Paul Gallant, and Joanne D. Eisen, "Is Resisting Genocide a Human Right?" *Notre Dame Law Review* 81, no. 4 (2006), https://scholarship.law.nd.edu/cgi/viewcontent.cgi?article=1347&context=ndlr.

330 Joseph Story, *A Familiar Exposition of the Constitution of the United States* (1847), §450.

331 Adolf Hitler, *Hitler's Table Talk, 1941–1944: His Private Conversations* H. R. Trevor-Roper and Norman Cameron, trans., (New York: Enigma Books, 2008), 321. Some controversy surrounds *Hitler's Table Talk*, particularly regarding the reliability of the English translation. But even historians who have raised concerns say that the manuscripts are based on genuine notes taken by secretaries to Hitler. One of those secretaries, Henry Picker, published the first edition of the *Table Talk*

DISARMED

in 1951, in the original German." Historian Richard Carrier of Columbia University reports that Picker's edition "carries the strongest claim to authenticity." (Richard C. Carrier, "'Hitler's Table Talk': Troubling Finds," *German Studies Review* 26, no. 3 [October 2003], https://www.jstor.org/stable/1432747). The quotation in question appears in Picker's edition as follows: "*Der größte Unsinn, den man in den besetzten Ostgebieten machen könne, sei der, den unterworfenen Völkern Waffen zu geben. Die Geschichte lehre, daß alle Herrenvölker untergegangen seien, nachdem sie den von ihnen unterworfenen Völkern Waffen bewilligt hätten. Ja, man könne geradezu sagen, daß die Auslieferung von Waffen an die unterworfenen Völker eine Conditio sine qua non für den Untergang der Herrenvölker sei.*" (Henry Picker, *Hitlers Tischgespräche im Führerhauptquartier* [Munich, Germany: Hockebooks, 2014], https://www.google.com/books/edition/Hitlers_Tischgespr%C3%A4che_im_F%C3%BChrerhauptq/VsMHAwAAQBAJ?hl=en&gbpv=0). Google Translate renders the passage as: "The greatest nonsense that could be done in the occupied eastern territories was to give arms to the conquered peoples. History teaches that all master nations perished after they had granted arms to the peoples they subjugated. Yes, one could actually say that the handing over of arms to the subjugated peoples was a condition sine qua non for the downfall of the master peoples." As rough as this translation may be, it conveys that Hitler indeed spoke about the dangers of letting subjugated people keep arms.

332 Austin Prochko, "Armed Populace Serves as Check on Government Overreach," *Washington Times*, June 20, 2022, https://www.washingtontimes.com/news/2022/jun/20/armed-populace-serves-as-check-on-government-overr/.

333 David B. Kopel, "Guns Kill People, and Tyrants with Gun Monopolies Kill the Most."

334 Kate Egner Gruber, "The Gunpowder Incident," American Battlefield Trust, https://www.battlefields.org/learn/articles/gunpowder-incident.

335 David B. Kopel, "The American Revolution Against British Gun Control," *Administrative and Regulatory Law News* (American Bar Association) 37, no. 4 (Summer 2012), https://davekopel.org/2A/LawRev/american-revolution-against-british-gun-control.html.

336 Quoted in Stephen P. Halbook, "'The Arms of All the People Should Be Taken Away,'" Independent Institute, January 1, 1989, https://www.independent.org/publications/article.asp?id=1422.

337 Quoted in Halbook, "'The Arms of All the People Should Be Taken Away.'"

338 Kopel, "The American Revolution Against British Gun Control."

339 "The Haitōrei Edict," Japan's Samurai Revolution, https://samurairevolution.omeka.net/exhibits/show/jy/section2.

340 The Haitōrei Edict, Japan's Samurai Revolution.

341 The Haitōrei Edict, Japan's Samurai Revolution.

342 "Declaration of the Rights of the Laboring and Exploited People," Central Executive Committee, Seventeen Moments in Soviet History, January 16, 1918, https://soviethistory.msu.edu/1917-2/workers-organization/workers-organization-texts/7149-2/.

343 "Decree on the Surrender of Weapons." Council of People's Commissars, Museum of History of Russian Reform, December 10, 1918, http://museumreforms.ru/node/13766.

344 Anne Applebaum, *Gulag: A History* (New York: Knopf, 2007), xvii.

345 Aleksandr Solzhenitsyn, The Gulag Archipelago, 1918–1956: An Experiment in Literary Investigation, I–II (Glasgow: Collins/Fontana, 1974), 13.

346 Yuri M. Zhukov, "Taking Away the Guns: Forcible Disarmament and Rebellion," *Journal of Peace Research* 53, no. 2 (March 2016), https://scholar.harvard.edu/files/zhukov/files/2015_zhukov_jpr_preprint.pdf.

347 Robert Conquest, *The Harvest of Sorrow: Soviet Collectivization and the Terror-Famine* (New York: Oxford University Press, 1986), 154.

348 David B. Kopel, Paul Gallant, and Joanne D. Eisen, "Firearms Possession by 'Non-State Actors': The Question of Sovereignty," *Texas Review of Law and Politics* 8, no. 2 (Spring 2004), available at SSRN, https://papers.ssrn.com/sol3/papers.cfm?abstract_id=742647.

349 Kopel, "Guns Kill People, and Tyrants with Gun Monopolies Kill the Most."

350 Kopel, "Guns Kill People, and Tyrants with Gun Monopolies Kill the Most."

351 David Kopel, "Data on Mass Murder by Government in the 20th Century," *Reason*, November 9, 2022, https://reason.com/volokh/2022/11/09/data-on-mass-murder-by-government-in-the-20th-century/.

352 Kopel, "Guns Kill People, and Tyrants with Gun Monopolies Kill the Most"; Kopel, Gallant, and Eisen, "Is Resisting Genocide a Human Right?"

353 Hollie McKay, "Venezuelans Regret Gun Ban, 'A Declaration of War Against an Unarmed Population,'" Fox News, December 14, 2018, https://www.foxnews.com/world/venezuelans-regret-gun-prohibition-we-could-have-defended-ourselves.

354 McKay, "Venezuelans Regret Gun Ban"; José Niño, "Gun Control Preceded the Tyranny in Venezuela," Foundation for Economic Education, January 22, 2019, https://fee.org/articles/gun-control-preceded-the-tyranny-in-venezuela/.

355 Anatoly Kurmanaev, "Terrorist Group Steps into Venezuela as Lawlessness Grows," *New York Times*, April 26, 2021, https://www.nytimes.com/2021/04/26/world/americas/venezuela-terrorist-colombia-ELN.html.

356 *Global Law and Order 2022*, report, Gallup, https://bluesyemre.files.wordpress.com/2022/10/2022-global-law-and-order-report.pdf.

357 McKay, "Venezuelans Regret Gun Ban."

358 Story, *A Familiar Exposition of the Constitution of the United States*, §450.

359 Sanford Levinson, "The Embarrassing Second Amendment."

360 Kopel, Gallant, and Eisen, "Firearms Possession by 'Non-State Actors.'"

361 Fred Frommer, "When Soviet-Led Forces Crushed the 1968 'Prague Spring,'" History.com, March 14, 2022, https://www.history.com/news/prague-spring-czechoslovakia-soviet-union.

362 Dr. Geraint Hughes, "The End of the Prague Spring—Fifty Years On," Defence-in-Depth, King's College London, August 20, 2018, https://defenceindepth.co/2018/08/20/the-end-of-the-prague-spring-fifty-years-on/.

363 Malcolm Byrne, Csaba Békés, and János M. Ranier, eds., *The 1956 Hungarian Revolution: A History in Documents* (Budapest: CEU Press, 2002), https://nsarchive2.gwu.edu/NSAEBB/NSAEBB76/.

364 Byrne, Békés, and Rainer, eds., *The 1956 Hungarian Revolution*.

365 "Report of the Special Committee on the Problem of Hungary," United Nations General Assembly Official Records: Eleventh Session Supplement No. 18 (A/3592), New York, 1957, http://mek.oszk.hu/01200/01274/01274.pdf.

366 Andor Keller, "No More Comrades," in William E. Morris and Richard Lettis, eds., *The Hungarian Revolt: October 23–November 4, 1956* (New York: Scribner, 1961), https://web.

archive.org/web/20061108181307/http://historicaltextarchive. com/books.php?op=viewbook&bookid=13&cid=15#N_1_.

367 Kopel, Gallant, and Eisen, "Firearms Possession by 'Non-State Actors.'"

368 Włodzimierz Borodziej, *The Warsaw Uprising of 1944*, Barbara Harshav, trans., (Madison: University of Wisconsin Press, 2001), 67.

369 Borodziej, *The Warsaw Uprising of 1944*, 155n16

370 Borodziej, *The Warsaw Uprising of 1944*, 67.

371 Borodziej, *The Warsaw Uprising of 1944*, 155n18.

372 Borodziej, *The Warsaw Uprising of 1944*, 67.

373 Jennifer Mascia, "That Time the NRA Tied the Tiananmen Square Massacre to American Gun Rights." The Trace, July 1, 2016, https://www.thetrace.org/2016/07/nra-tiananmen-square-ads-american-gun-rights/.

374 Nicholas J. Johnson, "Beyond the Second Amendment: An Individual Right to Arms Viewed through the Ninth Amendment," *Rutgers Law Journal* 24, no. 1 (Fall 1992), https://ir.lawnet.fordham.edu/cgi/viewcontent.cgi?referer=&httpsredir=1&article=1435&context=faculty_scholarship.

375 David B. Kopel, "Fewer Guns, More Genocide: Europe in the Twentieth Century," in Nicholas J. Johnson, David B. Kopel, George A. Mocsary, E. Gregory Wallace, and Donald Kilmer, *Firearms Law and the Second Amendment: Regulation, Rights, and Policy*, 3rd ed. (Boston: Aspen Publishing, 2022), http://firearmsregulation.org/www/FRRP3d_Ch19.pdf.

376 David B. Kopel, "The Party Commands the Gun: Mao Zedong's Arms Policies and Mass Killings," in Johnson, Kopel, Mocsary, Wallace, and Kilmer, *Firearms Law and the Second Amendment: Regulation, Rights, and Policy*.

377 Kopel, "Fewer Guns, More Genocide."

378 George Packer, "Ukrainians Are Defending the Values Americans Claim to Hold."

379 Jacqueline Howard, "US Records Highest Increase in Nation's Homicide Rate in Modern History, CDC Says," CNN, October 6, 2021, https://www.cnn.com/2021/10/06/health/us-homicide-rate-increase-nchs-study/index.html; John Gramlich, "What We Know About the Increase in U.S. Murders in 2020," Pew Research Center, October 27, 2021, https://www.pewresearch.org/fact-tank/2021/10/27/what-we-know-about-the-increase-in-u-s-murders-in-2020/.

380 Rachel E. Morgan, PhD, and Alexandra Thompson, "Criminal Victimization, 2020," Bureau of Justice Statistics, October 2021, Table 1, https://bjs.ojp.gov/sites/g/files/xyckuh236/files/media/document/cv20.pdf.

381 Jason Johnson, "Why Violent Crime Surged After Police Across America Retreated," *USA Today*, April 9, 2021, https://www.usatoday.com/story/opinion/policing/2021/04/09/violent-crime-surged-across-america-after-police-retreated-column/7137565002/.

382 Johnson, "Why Violent Crime Surged After Police Across America Retreated."

383 Johnson, "Why Violent Crime Surged After Police Across America Retreated."

384 Bill Hutchinson, "'It's Just Crazy': 12 Major Cities Hit All-Time Homicide Records," ABC News, December 8, 2021, https://abcnews.go.com/US/12-major-us-cities-top-annual-homicide-records/story?id=81466453.

385 "Recidivism," National Institute of Justice, U.S. Department of Justice, https://nij.ojp.gov/topics/corrections/recidivism; Liz Benecchi, "Recidivism Imprisons American Progress," *Harvard Political Review*, August 8, 2021, https://harvardpolitics.com/recidivism-american-progress/; Eva Herscowitz/TCR Staff, "US Recidivism Rates Stay Sky High," Crime Report, July 30, 2021, https://thecrimereport.org/2021/07/30/us-recidivism-rates-stay-sky-high/.

386 "Violent Crime," FBI, https://www.fbi.gov/investigate/violent-crime; *2015 National Gang Report*, National Gang Intelligence Center, FBI, https://www.gangenforcement.com/uploads/2/9/4/1/29411337/2015_-_national_gang_report.pdf.

387 See historical data in "National Youth Gang Survey Analysis: Measuring the Extent of Gang Problems," National Gang Center, https://nationalgangcenter.ojp.gov/survey-analysis/measuring-the-extent-of-gang-problems.

388 "National Youth Gang Survey Analysis: Gang-Related Offenses," National Gang Center, https://nationalgangcenter.ojp.gov/survey-analysis/gang-related-offenses.

389 "National Youth Gang Survey Analysis: Measuring the Extent of Gang Problems."

390 Richard Berk, "What Is a Mass Shooting? What Can Be Done?" University of Pennsylvania Department of Criminology, https://crim.sas.upenn.edu/fact-check/what-mass-shooting-what-can-be-done-0.

391 "11 Facts About Gangs," DoSomething.org, https://www.dosomething.org/us/facts/11-facts-about-gangs.

392 "National Youth Gang Survey Analysis: Measuring the Extent of Gang Problems."

393 Jennifer J. Adams and Jesenia M. Pizarro, "MS-13: A Gang Profile," *Journal of Gang Research* 16, no. 4 (Summer 2009), https://asu.pure.elsevier.com/en/publications/ms-13-a-gang-profile.

394 Sudhin Thanawala, "MS-13 Gang Used California Farm Town as a Base for Crime," Associated Press, August 31, 2018, https://apnews.com/article/291dd10b01374b038731ddb0eaa7d669; Matthew Ormseth, "A Place to Sleep, Party and Kill: Abandoned L.A. Buildings Become MS-13 Gang 'Destroyers,'" *Los Angeles Times*, July 7, 2021, https://www.latimes.com/california/story/2021-07-07/abandoned-la-building-ms-13-destroyer-killings.

395 Benjamin Weiser, "14 Gang Leaders Directed MS-13 'Wave of Death,' U.S. Says," *New York Times*, January 14, 2021, https://www.nytimes.com/2021/01/14/nyregion/ms-13-salvador-leaders-ranfla-nacional.html.

396 "Full-Scale Response: A Report on the Department of Justice's Efforts to Combat MS-13 from 2016 to 2020," U.S. Department of Justice, https://www.justice.gov/archives/ag/page/file/1329776/download.

397 Camilo Montoya-Galvez, "The Facts Behind the High Number of Migrants Arriving at the Border Under Biden," CBS News, August 31, 2022, https://www.cbsnews.com/news/immigration-biden-us-mexico-border/; "Southwest Land Border Encounters," U.S. Customs and Border Protection, https://www.cbp.gov/newsroom/stats/southwest-land-border-encounters.

398 "Criminal Noncitizen Statistics Fiscal Year 2022," U.S. Customs and Border Protection, https://www.cbp.gov/newsroom/stats/cbp-enforcement-statistics/criminal-noncitizen-statistics; Andrew Mark Miller, "Crimes Committed by Illegal Immigrants Surged in 2021 After Declining in Previous Years," Fox News, July 7, 2022, https://www.foxnews.com/us/crimes-committed-illegal-immigrants-surged-2021-declining-previous-years.

399 John Feng, "Three in 10 Americans Believe U.S. Will Be Invaded Within 10 Years: Poll."

400 Feng, "Three in 10 Americans Believe U.S. Will Be Invaded Within 10 Years: Poll."

401 Vivian Giang, "Banking Turmoil: What We Know, New York Times," March 14, 2023, https://www.nytimes.com/article/svb-silicon-valley-bank-explainer.html

402 Patrick J. Kiger, "How Venezuela Fell from the Richest Country in South America into Crisis," History.com, May 9, 2019, https://www.history.com/news/venezuela-chavez-maduro-crisis; Tim Padgett, "The Disaster That Is Venezuela," *New York Times*, March 15, 2022, https://www.nytimes.com/2022/03/15/books/review/things-are-never-so-bad-that-they-cant-get-worse-venezuela-william-neuman.html; Kurmanaev, "Terrorist Group Steps into Venezuela as Lawlessness Grows"; "GDP Per Capita (Current US$)—Venezuela, RB," World Bank, https://data.worldbank.org/indicator/NY.GDP.PCAP.CD?locations=VE.

403 David Harsanyi, "Bloomberg: Guns for Me, but Not for Thee," *National Review*, March 3, 2020, https://www.nationalreview.com/2020/03/michael-bloomberg-guns-for-me-but-not-for-thee/.

404 Cheryl K. Chumley, "NYC's Michael Bloomberg Accused of 'Hypocrisy' for Arming Security Detail in Gun-Free Bermuda," *Washington Times*, March 26, 2013, https://www.washingtontimes.com/news/2013/mar/26/nycs-michael-bloomberg-accused-hypocrisy-arming-se/.

405 Marcus Gilmer, "In Post About Las Vegas Shooting, Mark Zuckerberg Addresses Gun Control Debate," Mashable, October 2, 2017, https://mashable.com/2017/10/02/zuckerberg-statement-las-vegas-shooting/#BhL9Hh55C5qQ.

406 "Terms and Policies: Prohibited Content: Weapons, Ammunition, or Explosives," Meta, https://www.facebook.com/policies_center/ads/prohibited_content/weapons.

407 Phil Matier and Andy Ross, "Mark Zuckerberg's Social Network Includes 24-Hour Security," *San Francisco Chronicle*, September 18, 2015, https://www.sfchronicle.com/bayarea/matier-ross/article/Mark-Zuckerberg-s-social-network-includes-6515603.php.

408 Joyce Chen, "All About Mark Zuckerberg's Expansive, High-Tech Real Estate Holdings," *Architectural Digest*, February 24, 2022, https://www.architecturaldigest.com/story/zuckerberg-real-estate-holdings.

409 See Cesare Beccaria, *An Essay on Crimes and Punishments, translated from the Italian with a commentary, attributed to M. de Voltaire, translated from the French* (New York: Stephen Gould, 1809), 124–25.

410 John D. Bessler, "The Italian Enlightenment and the American Revolution: Cesare Beccaria's Forgotten Influence on American Law," *Mitchell Hamline Law Journal of Public Policy and Practice* 37, no. 1 (2016): 5.

411 Report on Books for Congress, Papers of James Madison at the Library of Congress, January 23, 1783.

412 Bernard E. Harcourt, "Beccaria's 'On Crimes and Punishments': A Mirror on the History of the Foundations of Modern Criminal Law," *Chicago Unbound* 4 (2013), https://chicagounbound.uchicago.edu/cgi/viewcontent.cgi?article=1633&context=law_and_economics.

413 Beccaria, *An Essay on Crimes and Punishments*, 124–25.

414 Beccaria, *An Essay on Crimes and Punishments*, 124–25.

415 Quoted in Stephen P. Halbrook, "What the Framers Intended: A Linguistic Analysis of the Right to Bear Arms," *Law and Contemporary Problems* 49, no. 1 (Winter 1986): 154, https://scholarship.law.duke.edu/cgi/viewcontent.cgi?article=3830&context=lcp.

416 Quoted in Halbrook, "What the Framers Intended."

417 Hollie McKay, "Ukrainians Start Arming Themselves for Possible Russian Attack."

418 Stephen P. Halbrook, America's Rifle: The Case for the AR-15 (Post-Hill Press 2022).

419 Patrick Henry, Remarks to the Second Virginia Convention, St. John's Church, Richmond, Virginia, March 23, 1775, https://www.colonialwilliamsburg.org/learn/deep-dives/give-me-liberty-or-give-me-death/.

420 Henry, Remarks to the Second Virginia Convention.

421 Noah Webster, "An Examination of the Leading Principles of the Federal Constitution," October 17, 1787, in *The Constitution and Other Documents of the Founding Fathers* (New York: Race Point Publishing, 2017), 123.

422 Story, *Commentaries on the Constitution* (1833), 3:§1890.

423 "An Act for Amending the Several Laws for Regulating and Disciplining the Militia, and Guarding Against Invasions and Insurrections," in *Military Obligation: The American Tradition*, vol. 2, part 14, *Virginia Enactments*, 422–25.

424 The Editorial Board, "New York's 'Massive Resistance' to the Supreme Court on Guns," *Wall Street Journal*, July

4, 2022, https://www.wsj.com/articles/new-yorks-massive-resistance-to-the-supreme-court-kathy-hochul-clarence-thomas-albany-guns-bruen-11656893336.

425. Andrew Fletcher, *A Discourse of Government with Relation to Militias* (1698), at "Andrew Fletcher: Selected Discourses and Speeches," Liberty Fund, https://oll.libertyfund.org/title/fletcher-selected-discourses-and-speeches.

426. The Trace does little to hide its bias in favor of gun control. The organization also received its initial funding from Michael Bloomberg's anti-gun organization Everytown for Gun Safety. See Michael Calderone, "The Trace, Bloomberg-Backed Journalism Startup, Tackles Gun Violence 'Epidemic,'" *Huffington Post*, June 16, 2015, https://www.huffpost.com/entry/the-trace-bloomberg-guns_n_7581446.

427. "From Negro Militias to Black Armament," *Code Switch*, NPR, December 22, 2020, https://www.npr.org/sections/codeswitch/2020/12/22/949169826/from-negro-militias-to-black-armament.

428. *Dred Scott v. Sandford*, 60 U.S. 393 (1857), https://www.oyez.org/cases/1850-1900/60us393.

429. See Stephen Halbrook, "The Second Amendment Was Adopted to Protect Liberty, Not Slavery: A Reply to Professors Bogus and Anderson," 20 Georgetown Journal of Law & Public Policy 575 (Summer 2022).

430. Nicholas Johnson, "The Arming and Disarming of Black America," *Slate*, February 10, 2018, https://

slate.com/human-interest/2018/02/what-reconstruction-and-its-end-meant-for-black-americans-who-had-fought-for-the-right-to-keep-and-bear-arms.html.

431 Quoted in Johnson, "The Arming and Disarming of Black America."

432 David B. Kopel, "The Racist Roots of Gun Control," Encounter Books, February 23, 2018, https://www.encounterbooks.com/features/racist-roots-gun-control/.

433 *The Liberator*, June 5, 1863, quoted in "Ballot Box, Jury Box, Cartridge Box," Quote Investigator, https://quoteinvestigator.com/2018/04/09/ballot/.

434 Frederick Douglass, *The Life and Times of Frederick Douglass* (Mineola, NY: Dover Publications, 2012), 275.

435 *New York State Rifle & Pistol Association, Inc. v. Bruen*, 597 U.S. ___ (2022), https://supreme.justia.com/cases/federal/us/597/20-843/.

436 Jacob Sullum, "Why Martin Luther King Couldn't Get a Carry Permit," *Reason*, October 27, 2021, https://reason.com/2021/10/27/why-martin-luther-king-couldnt-get-a-carry-permit/.

437 David L. Stern and Robyn Dixon, "Ukraine's Zelensky's Message Is Don't Panic. That's Making the West Antsy," *Washington Post*, February 7, 2022, https://www.washingtonpost.com/world/2022/01/30/ukraine-zelensky-russia-biden/.

438 Shane Harris, Karen DeYoung, Isabelle Khurshudyan, Ashley Parker, and Liz Sly, "Road to War: U.S. Struggled to Convince Allies, and Zelensky, of Risk of Invasion."

439 Harris, DeYoung, Khurshudyan, Parker, and Sly, "Road to War"; Mark F. Cancian, "Putin's Invasion Was Immoral but Not Irrational," Center for Strategic and International Studies, May 10, 2022, https://www.csis.org/analysis/putins-invasion-was-immoral-not-irrational.

440 Anthony S. Pitch, *The Burning of Washington: The British Invasion of 1814* (Annapolis: Naval Institute Press, 1998), 99-152, 205-216.

441 Pitch, *The Burning of Washington*, 226-34.

442 The Editors of Encyclopedia Britannica, "Mexican-American War," *Encyclopedia Britannica*, https://www.britannica.com/event/Mexican-American-War.

443 "Pancho Villa," History.com, August 21, 2018, https://www.history.com/topics/latin-america/pancho-villa.

444 Samuel J. Cox, "H-010-6: Attacks on the U.S. Mainland in World War I and World War II," Naval History and Heritage Command, https://www.history.navy.mil/about-us/leadership/director/directors-corner/h-grams/h-gram-010/h-010-6.html.

445 HistroyNet Staff, "Japanese Submarines Prowl the U.S. Pacific Coastline in 1941," HistoryNet, June 12, 2006, https://www.historynet.com/japanese-submarines-prowl-the-us-pacific-coastline-in-1941/.

446 Evan Andrews, "5 Attacks on U.S. Soil During World War II," History.com, August 30, 2018, https://www.history.com/news/5-attacks-on-u-s-soil-during-world-war-ii.

447 Andrews, "5 Attacks on U.S. Soil During World War II."

448 "Battle of Attu: 60 Years Later," National Park Service, https://www.nps.gov/articles/000/battle-of-attu-60-years.htm.

449 Andrews, "5 Attacks on U.S. Soil During World War II."

450 "Saudi Arabia, home to 15 of the 19 September 11 hijackers, is keen to show how much has changed," CBS News, September 10, 2021, https://www.cbsnews.com/news/saudi-arabia-shows-anti-extremism-terrorism-efforts-9-11-anniversary/.

451 Mark F. Cancian, "Avoiding Coping with Surprise in Great Power Conflicts," Center for Strategic and International Studies, February 2018, https://www.csis.org/analysis/coping-surprise-great-power-conflicts.

452 Cancian, "Putin's Invasion Was Immoral but Not Irrational."

453 Cancian, "Avoiding Coping with Surprise in Great Power Conflicts."

454 See, e.g., Matthew Knott, "Joe Biden Supports Australian-Style Gun Buyback Scheme After Massacres," *Sydney Morning Herald* (Australia), August 7, 2019, https://www.smh.com.au/world/north-america/joe-biden-supports-australian-style-gun-buyback-scheme-after-massacres-20190807-p52el4.html; Helen Davidson, "Obama Backs Australia's Gun Laws While Condemning Latest Mass Shootings in US," *The Guardian* (UK), June 23, 2015, https://www.theguardian.com/

us-news/2015/jun/23/obama-backs-australias-gun-laws-while-condemning-latest-mass-shootings-in-us; Bradford Richardson "Hillary: Australia-Style Gun Control 'Worth Looking At,'" *The Hill*, October 16, 2015, https://thehill.com/blogs/ballot-box/dem-primaries/257172-hillary-australia-style-gun-control-worth-looking-at/; Zack Beauchamp, "Australia Confiscated 650,000 Guns. Murders and Suicides Plummeted," Vox, May 25, 2022, https://www.vox.com/2015/8/27/9212725/australia-buyback; Max Fisher, "Other Countries Had Mass Shootings. Then They Changed Their Gun Laws," *New York Times*, May 25, 2022, https://www.nytimes.com/2022/05/25/world/europe/gun-laws-australia-britain.html.

455 Mogelson, "How Ukrainians Saved Their Capital.".

456 Giulia Heyward, "Trudeau Orders an Immediate Freeze on the Sale of Handguns in Canada," NPR, October 21, 2022, https://www.npr.org/2022/10/21/1130608885/justin-trudeau-canada-handgun-sales-freeze.

457 Mogelson, "How Ukrainians Saved Their Capital."

458 Packer, "Ukrainians Are Defending the Values Americans Claim to Hold."

459 Judge Alex Kozinski, dissent, *Silveira v. Lockyer*, 328 F. 3d 567 (2003), U.S. Court of Appeals, 9th Circuit, https://scholar.google.com/scholar_case?case=16599538532304446493.

460 Kozinski, dissent, *Silveira v. Lockyer*.

461 Kozinski, dissent, *Silveira v. Lockyer*.

DISARMED

ABOUT THE AUTHOR

Mark W. Smith is a constitutional attorney, a member of the U.S. Supreme Court Bar and a *New York Times* bestselling author. He is the creator and host of *The Four Boxes Diner* program, a popular YouTube channel providing legal and scholarly analysis of the Second Amendment, the right to bear arms and more. Mark is a Distinguished Scholar at the Ave Maria School of Law and a Presidential Scholar at The King's College. Mark graduated from the NYU School of Law. His Twitter handle is @FourBoxesDiner

Made in the USA
Las Vegas, NV
07 September 2023